THE METAVERSE

TERRY WINTERS

THE METAVERSE

PREPARE NOW FOR THE NEXT BIG THING

Terry Winters Media

CONTENTS

FOREWORD

As the next era of the Internet, the metaverse is projected to deliver a digital environment more reminiscent of real life and has been heralded as a logical successor to Web 2.0 content platforms, 2D interfaces, and centralized virtual role-playing worlds like Second Life[1].

Existing in parallel to reality, and in some, cases, overlapping the physical world, the metaverse will allow people to work, open businesses, socialize, communicate, and interact with one another in a fully immersive solar system of virtual destinations. Some commentators even liken the metaverse to being inside the Internet rather than simply looking at it from a phone or computer screen.

Naturally, many people have doubts about the metaverse and it's easy to see why. Fused with science fiction and nascent technology, life in a virtual world defies and challenges core notions of what it is to be human. The promise of a metaverse also raises ethical concerns and unending existential questions. Is the metaverse real? Will it happen? If so, how will we use it? Who will be the first adopters? Does current technology make it possible? What problems might arise from its existence? Who will profit from its existence? How will it impact children and people's ability to socialize in the real world? And, of course, how can I make money from it...?

These are some of the questions we need to ask and answer before we outright dismiss the metaverse as a passing fad or science fiction. For those who followed the commercial let-down of Google Glass last decade, head-mounted display technology conjures residual doubt and skepticism, but augmented reality (AR) is just one piece of the complex metaverse jigsaw. Other adjoining pieces are clicking into place, with blockchain technology, virtual reality (VR), artificial intelligence (AI), 5G Internet, remote work, and online social activities accelerated by a global pandemic. Together, these technologies and trends are converging to construct a virtual universe in the form of the metaverse, and augmented reality will likely be a core part of its overall development.

For VR technology, there is a similar uphill battle to achieving mass adoption after many rounds of underwhelming attempts. You might have heard of Oculus Rift from a decade ago but virtual reality dates all the way back to 1968. While some attempts were nothing more than basic prototypes, including the first functional head-mounted VR system called the Sword of Damocles[2] (that was suspended from the ceiling), other projects managed to peek into the virtual entertainment market with arcade-style games like Atari's Battlezone (1980) and Nintendo's Virtual Boy (1995). However, it wasn't until recently that consumer-grade VR made a real push towards mainstream adoption and exposure, beginning with Oculus Rift's Kickstarter campaign at the end of 2012.

Now, with the advent of 5G Internet, the launch of Facebook's metaverse world called Horizon Worlds, and mass digital adoption driven by COVID-19, we finally find ourselves on the verge of something big and potentially paradigm-shifting with regards to VR technology.

Advanced VR and AR will allow us to generate attention to a brand, business, community, or cultural cause in a way that wasn't possible before. This includes designing virtual games layered on the real world using augmented reality, opening a virtual 3D mall, buying and flipping virtual land, or unveiling your own

3D art gallery. The potential business value contained in VR and AR applications in the metaverse will very likely outweigh the costs of past attempts.

Still, deep insights on this new era of the metaverse and the accompanying technology remain in short supply. Understanding the various moving components, platforms, and technologies powering the metaverse demands time and research to fully understand. By publishing this book, I hope to share my knowledge and research on the metaverse and connect with other enthusiasts to compare notes and share knowledge about projects as well as other opportunities to co-create valuable services and experiences in the metaverse. (Reach out to me via Twitter **terrywinters07** or email **terrywinters@protonmail.com**)

Indeed, one of the most exciting prospects of the metaverse is the open invitation to participate and invest in its development, including the ability to invest in new projects, create user-generated content, and participate in decentralized autonomous organizations (DAOs).

By voting, sharing, and buying assets or currencies in a virtual world, individuals have the potential to shape projects just like first and second-round investors did in startups like Tesla and Facebook well before these companies went public. Additionally, the metaverse will become a great source of inspiration for artists, game developers, architects, and many other professionals to share their creativity and vision of the future.

While the development of the metaverse is already underway, there are no sure bets on which projects will survive and thrive in this new iteration of the virtual economy. At present, investments can only be directed to individual projects and not in the overall metaverse as a broad single bet. There are no metaverse ETFs (exchange-traded funds) that include decentralized projects (where decision-making is dispersed across a network of actors and not controlled by a central organization/individual/group), no single metaverse currency, and no global metaverse entity. As a consequence, you need to be vigilant in choosing where you allocate and invest your capital—whether that's investing a hundred dollars in virtual trainers or tens of thousands of dollars in virtual property.

It's also very likely that the term "the metaverse" will be deployed as a buzzword like big data, AI, or IoT to attract hyped-up investments for startups as well as encourage unsuspected victims into Ponzi schemes that overdeliver on their vision and fail to deliver on promised results. On top of this, the metaverse tends to invoke an optimistic and utopian view of the future—especially given its roots in science fiction and cyberpunk literature.

Like a savvy angel investor, you will need to tread carefully in this space, conduct your own extensive research, and form your own hypotheses for deciding which projects to back and why. This will probably include careful analysis of network effects, gamification, business opportunities, communities, new technology, as well as networking with other investors and maybe meeting the founders of projects (in the metaverse) to extrapolate the future value of different worlds.

Alternatively, if you don't have the disposable income to invest, and are skeptical of virtual land or resistant to the get-rich-quick culture of crypto-related projects, there are other opportunities to combine real-world connections and expertise to find work, highlight important issues, and provide value to other participants in the metaverse. This includes becoming a virtual educator, event organizer, or spokesperson on important issues at virtual events. Or perhaps you're an avid gamer, especially massively multiplayer online (MMO) games, you understand virtual ownership, and you want to learn more about what blockchain technology has to offer in order to start a new path in Indie game development. Conversely, maybe you want to set up a construction company, architecture firm, marketing agency, or events company as a service provider in the metaverse.

For those who want to gain practical experience with web3 tools including cryptocurrency wallets, the Appendix of this book includes a Getting Started guide and further recommended resources are also included at the end of the book.

I also want to emphasize that the metaverse is not for everyone and that's okay. You don't have to spend time there or buy virtual land and other virtual assets. Much like the first era of the Internet, part of the metaverse's attraction is that it sits outside the traditional edges of reality and therein offers an alternative medium for people to socialize, work, invest, or explore. In fact, people confined or marginalized by reality are likely to be the first adopters of virtual experiences in the metaverse, and those content with reality may not see the need to sign into any metaverse world. At the very least, it's valuable to understand your options and be aware of what the metaverse might one day offer and before deciding if this is an area of interest you wish to explore further in the future.

Lastly, nothing in this book constitutes legal, tax, or investment advice. Always conduct your own research. Also note that information about projects, including names, leaders, and product offerings, are subject to change in the future.

DEFINING THE METAVERSE

The online economy and community are growing at an explosive rate. While the Internet was once received with resistance and disbelief, there are now billions of active users with a daily presence on an assortment of social media sites. It's also difficult to turn off the Internet thanks to fast broadband connections, Internet-enabled smartphones, and access through ubiquitous browsers.

Much of the current state of the Internet falls under the framework of Web 2.0, which came into prominence around 2004 for describing a new evolution of the web, orientated towards user-generated content and interactivity.

Web 2.0 succeeds Web 1.0 (developed in the 1990s), which can be understood as the informational replacement of traditional print media such as newspapers, magazines and books as well as radio, TV, and movies that relied on HTML to provide information via text. During this period, the web was comparatively open as companies deployed content on their own website rather than secondary platforms such as social media and e-commerce websites that could potentially shut down their access at any time. Interactions on the Internet, though, were limited. The emergence of Web 2.0 later emphasized the use of multimedia and collaboration between web users to encourage user interactions and create an online environment rich in media content. Examples of some successful Web 2.0 applications include Facebook, Reddit, YouTube, and Twitter.

As the next development phase of the Internet, web3 is expected to change the landscape once again. This natural evolution of the Internet is assembled around decentralization and peer-to-peer networks linked on the blockchain in place of the centrally owned, managed, and regulated web applications we currently know and use today. Web3's emphasis on decentralization is grounded on the idea that "users are the platform" and the platform is sustained collectively by those who take part in it. As part-owners of the platform, users are therefore entitled to enjoy sovereignty over their virtual assets, data, and digital wealth.

This transformation in infrastructure and drive towards user-centricity is already giving rise to brand new applications including decentralized finance (DiFi)[3] and reviving unrealized ideas such as the metaverse.

The grand vision of the metaverse is to provide a parallel digital universe connected to our physical world through multiple digital technologies. These parallel virtual environments and the convergence of the online and offline worlds will allow us to experience and communicate in the digital world through avatars—the user's chosen persona—and feature many elements from physical reality including buildings, work and leisure locations, and other different landscapes. Many of these metaverse worlds will consist of limited land; land that you can build on, lease, and socialize with other avatars.

The ultimate goal of the metaverse is to look and feel like physical reality, allowing your avatar to move around freely, interact with others, and access information within a 3D environment just like in the real world. Interactions will affect both your own state of being and that of others in the metaverse. This means that the metaverse may offer us the opportunity to work remotely. By entering a virtual office environment on a regular or drop-in drop-out basis, it might be possible to spend part of our time working interactively and virtually from the comfort of our physical homes.

During the first year of the COVID-19 outbreak, three employees at a company in Japan trialed teleworking inside the game Animal Crossing, using one of the employee's islands as a virtual meeting location. While the social office experiment did not persist—due in part to deficits in the in-game communication tools—3D virtual locations do provide a promising future over traditional 2D calls.

Before we dive deeper into what business and work opportunities lie ahead, it's important to define and understand the original vision and origins of the metaverse.

At present, defining the metaverse is still not clear or universally agreed-upon given that it entails a vision of the future rather than something that already exists. Combining the prefix "meta" (meaning beyond) and "universe", the term was coined and popularized by science fiction author and journalist Neal Stephenson. In his 1992 cyberpunk novel Snow Crash, Stephenson imagined the metaverse as a collective and physically persistent virtual shared space connected to the real world rather than existing only in cyberspace.

Coined by William Gibson in his book "Neuromancer", cyberspace refers to the collective digital information space within any electronic medium. The terminology has been used to imply that the Internet represents another dimension in which physical laws do not apply, making the online space a world apart or distinct from everyday reality. The use of "cyber", meanwhile, has attempted to connote a synonym for virtual or computer network.

Unlike cyberspace, the metaverse aims to connect with reality by designing a large-scale virtual reality setting where anyone can have a persistent presence as an extension of their physical self or company. This, in a sense, provides an opportunity for participants to create their own virtual spaces that may represent physical places, such as a city square or park; imaginary places, such as a medieval castle; an online space, say a community room or video game environment, or even something else entirely and invite other people to participate.

The metaverse could also be a merger of all realities, filled with artificial intelligent entities, making it possible for people and other sentient beings to communicate and interact in shared environments as portrayed in the 2021 film Free Guy (with human players, role-playing characters, and AI-powered characters interacting in one interactive world).

Still, it is perhaps from Neal Stephenson where we find the best insight into what an eventual metaverse might look like. In Snow Crash, Neal Stephenson uses the term "the Metaverse" to describe a virtual reality environment built on multiple sensory inputs, including sight, sound, and smell. The lead character, Hiro, says of the Metaverse, "It was big and getting bigger all the time, like an expanding universe. Theoretically, there was no limit to how big the Metaverse could be."

In Snow Crash, the Metaverse constitutes an urban environment, constructed along a single hundred-meter-wide road, called the Street, which runs 65,536 km around a spherical planet. To gain access, visitors require physical hardware including virtual reality goggles and sound equipment to visit and interact with others through a first-person perspective. They access the Metaverse via personal computer terminals that project a high-quality VR display onto their goggles or through lower-quality public terminals located in booths.

When visitors log in, they are assigned an avatar, which is a graphical representation of their physical appearance (no taller than their height in real life). However, visitors that log in from public terminals can only appear in black-and-white.

The use of VR technology in Stephenson's novel is mostly restricted to instances where it makes economic sense; users typically cannot afford to wear the special equipment indefinitely so instead they log out after they've finished using it. However, Stephenson also describes a sub-group of people who choose to remain continuously connected to the Metaverse. These characters wear portable computer terminals, goggles, and other equipment and are nicknamed "gargoyles" in light of their so-called "grotesque" appearance.

In the Metaverse, each world is called a domain and has its own online laws, which are enforced by software agents known as "scrags" that monitor all activity. Visitors can be sent to jail in the Metaverse for breaking these rules and lose their avatars or become stuck there forever.

One region of the Metaverse is maintained by a private conglomerate known as the Central Intelligence Corporation, which owns most of the computer infrastructure and virtual land in this alternate Internet. Virtual land in the Metaverse is as valuable as real estate in Meatspace (the word Hiro uses for reality). This virtual land can be bought and sold by users who pay a monthly fee to maintain their private property rights.

Similar to the fictional domains described in Stephenson's Metaverse, our own metaverse probably won't consist of one single destination owned by Facebook or Google. It will, instead, be populated by many interconnected worlds and owned by a collection of different entities. These virtual worlds, whether e-commerce, social, or game-based will connect to underwrite the overarching metaverse.

Additionally, developing a virtual world-based game doesn't mean instant participation in the metaverse. As was the case in Snow Crash, a metaverse world must have the technical capacity to support user-generated content creation, permanent asset ownership, live interactions, scenes that don't automatically pause or reset, high numbers of concurrent users, and a multifaceted economy driven by consumer spending and independent businesses.

Dovetailing with its complex theoretical borders, the development of a true metaverse-like world also faces serious challenges including technology, as detailed in Chapter 3. Another major challenge is appealing to non-technology focused market segments, especially given the virtual worlds' reputation for being a geeky passing fad with little mainstream appeal or utility. While technophiles might embrace the idea of personal avatars in an online environment, virtual reality as a whole has historically been niche and unsuccessful compared to traditional Web 2.0 applications.

One of the other prominent complaints made against the metaverse is the fact that it won't fully replicate what can be experienced in the physical world, such as attending a live music concert or meeting a celebrity in the flesh. While this criticism is valid and there are limits to technology, it overlooks the vast majority of people today who are unable to experience live concerts in a far-away city or directly interact with their favorite idols. For famous people, the metaverse also offers a convenient and safe space to connect with fans and followers.

Just as communication through mobile phones has not fully replaced the need for people to meet face-to-face, the metaverse is not supposed to be a replacement or substitute for real-life experiences and interactions. Instead, it aims to help decentralize and distribute new opportunities to more people on the planet as what can be termed "the next best thing" for many people.

In this way, the metaverse opens a parallel world of opportunities for those less privileged by their immediate geography or economic circumstances. As Neal Stephenson writes in Snow Crash, "when you live in a shithole, there's always the Metaverse, and in the Metaverse, Hiro Protagonist is a warrior prince." In the real world, Hiro Protagonist lived with his cash-strapped friend in a cheap storage unit. Likewise, in the novel *Ready Player One* by Ernest Cline, the main protagonist had few real-world assets and logged in to the metaverse via an abandoned van.

The third challenge involves figuring out how interactions in the metaverse should work, especially in regards to content moderation. Is it okay to host a virtual event for extremist and dangerous organizations or to instigate a riot between members of racist groups? Will there be age-restricted content?

In Second Life, minors aged between 13 and 17 can access the platform but strict restrictions are in place on what content they can view. The Second Life world is also split into sections with their own assigned maturity level rating similar to movies, including General (for minors), Moderate, and Adult. However, there are few to no restrictions on content, actions, animations, and businesses within new metaverse projects today that is adult in nature.[4]

Next, if everyone can edit anything at any time, will it still be possible to create a coherent experience? Moreover, if nearly everything in the metaverse is user-generated, including games and videos, then not every object will be graphically optimized for mass distribution. In Second Life, it's not uncommon for users to consume compute power 12 times the amount needed for an equivalent visual result properly optimized in another game.

At this point, the only way to determine whether or not these issues are solvable is through iterative testing, community-based decision-making and governance, metaverse standards and ethics initiatives, and ongoing improvements.

Additionally, the proliferation of metaverse platforms may lead to the formation of a metaverse standard for interactions between virtual worlds. Such an interface would potentially support many types of interactions including fluid asset transferal, digital wallet integration, avatar movement and teleporting, e-commerce, currency exchange, and applications that allow users to

connect via 3D videoconferencing and instant or voice chat programs.

CREATING A NEW IDENTITY IN THE METAVERSE

As the metaverse grows and becomes more real, one of the first steps is to create and manage your digital identity or persona. This includes creating a consistent appearance, name, and mobile assets that you can take from one digital world to another—similar to how you do in the physical world.

In many ways, most people already have a shadow persona that exists on the Internet. This shadow persona is made up of crumbs of metadata deposited across the web, including numerous social media profiles, purchasing and gaming history, user-generated content, community badges, chat logs, karma, as well as in-game assets. This information however is technically owned and controlled by companies such as Facebook and Amazon and diffused across many centralized platforms.

Part of the promise of the metaverse is to reclaim ownership and sovereignty over your digital self through permanent ownership of your digital assets (as discussed in Chapter 4 vis-à-vis the blockchain and NFTs) and to consolidate your online interactions and records of metadata under a single and fluid digital identity. The transition from a fragmented shadow online presence to a digital avatar[5] includes having a pseudonym, digital clothing and accessories, and an appearance that conveys a certain personality and embodies your physical self in the digital world.

In gaming and virtual worlds, the term digital avatar can be described as a graphical representation of a person while also embodying some characteristics attributed to the person it is intended to represent. The graphical attributes of an avatar matter as they provide an indication of how others expect you to behave and how they know you virtually. The idea of what you wear digitally will also become an important decision as that again reflects your identity. For instance, when we see someone in real life wearing a suit, we expect them to behave and speak in a certain manner. We don't think this way about someone who is dressed casually in a hoodie, even though they are both humans. We have different expectations based on visual cues.

What we wear or look like in the digital world has also been found to affect how we behave in both the virtual and physical world based on how people typically associate certain characteristics. One Stanford University research project[6] by Nick Yee and Jeremy Bailensen in 2009 discovered The Proteus Effect[7], which describes a phenomenon in which the characteristics of an individual's avatar within a virtual world affects their social behavior. For example, the researchers found that participants with more attractive avatars in an immersive virtual environment were more intimate in regards to self-disclosure and were more willing to approach opposite-gendered strangers (within less than one minute of being assigned their avatar). In another experiment, they found that participants with taller avatars behaved more confidently in a negotiation task and were more willing to make unfair splits than participants with shorter avatars. Participants with shorter avatars, meanwhile, were comparatively more willing to accept unfair offers. Other studies by Bailensen have found that confidence garnered in the virtual world can also cross over into how people behave in the real world. This does, however, raise ask the question of whether negative experiences in the virtual world (including cyberbullying, defeat in a game, or redundancy) will carry over and affect one's self-esteem in the real world.

Another aspect of living through an avatar is the ability to sample new identities and personas online, different from one's offline persona but perhaps more authentic and truer to who they really are and with less fear of social repercussions. Some avatar characteristics may therefore differ dramatically from the actual personality and appearance of a person in real life, such as an introverted man interacting as an extroverted woman.

In balance, most people will probably choose an avatar that reflects some of their general characteristics, such as skin color and gender, but with some obvious enhancements to their aesthetic appearance. Avatars will also probably alter from platform to platform, especially as some worlds are voxel-based like Minecraft, graphics-based like Second Life, or 3D scans of the real world similar to Microsoft Flight Simulator. One interesting project in the 3D scanning and modeling technology space is MetaHero, which allows you to make ultra-realistic scans of yourself and port them into different metaverse worlds.

In terms of fashion, users can already create and don wearables like digital trainers (footwear) or skins (a graphic or audio download that modifies the appearance of an avatar) that they can trade as part of an elaborate virtual economy.

Another attractive part of building a life in the metaverse is constructing an identity around a pseudonym. Separate from your real name, pseudonyms are search-resistant identities that exist in the digital world, including the many millions of social media users posting content under assumed names. A real name, meanwhile, is a state name or a social security name that works as a global identifier, which governments, organizations, and even individuals can search in global databases. In the book *Seeing Like a State*, the author James C. Scott explains that historically, governments in many regions promoted a permanent last name system to facilitate taxation, conscription, and prevent rebellion by making it easier to find people.

Pseudonymity is also different from anonymity, which is a totally disposable identifier, as exercised on the website 4chan. The site has no registration and login process, meaning that posts are usually submitted under the default username "Anonymous".

Pseudonymity, therefore, provides an equilibrium between a real name identifier and complete anonymity. A pseudonym shields your identity online as it can't be easily linked to your home address, ID documentation, and employer, but is still persistent in nature, allowing you to accumulate reputation and relationships over time. In fact, your pseudonym might become more famous than your real name. This unlocks the path to enjoying the benefits of celebrity status without sharing your true identity and thereby adversely affecting family members and your neighbors. Virtual celebrities and influencers can avoid the burden of fans, the media, and bad actors knowing where they live in the physical world and gives them space to step back or step away from the spotlight.

After creating a new name that represents your avatar and which is intrinsic to your digital personality, you have the ability to earn digital income and acquire assets under that name without ever revealing your true identity. This digital guarantee offers employment opportunities for people regardless of their race, age, or physical appearance but poses many challenges as well.

While digital pseudonymity has been largely tolerated in the past and has played an important role in the development of the Internet, this convention is likely to clash with norms and regulations in the future. Governments, for example, will be wary of enforcing greater transparency in regards to shielding ownership of income and assets and especially as the digital economy multiplies and interacts with the broader mainstream economy.

Governments won't be alone in lobbying for greater transparency. Employers will be want to know what their employees are doing in the metaverse. In the wake of COVID-19, more employees around the world work remotely, which gives them ample opportunities to leverage their employer's software, intellectual property, and work hours to earn a secondary income in secret. Such an arrangement not only contravenes the employee's employment contract but potentially taxation laws that discriminate against secondary income.

The sum result is that employees' loyalty to one organization (who pays their income) is likely to diminish in the new era of the Internet. Governments, meanwhile, will need to reconsider how they tax multiple incomes to encourage citizens to volunteer their earning information for taxation purposes.

For individuals, there is a completely separate problem in regards to managing a pseudonym. As each virtual platform operates its own user registration system, it's difficult to claim a consistent name across multiple platforms and establish a permanent identity within the greater metaverse.

You might find your username available on one platform but the same username might be claimed on another platform. Also, even if you're quick to claim a valuable username across multiple platforms, you still need to keep your eyes on new platforms in case someone else claims your name and holds it for ransom or jeopardizes your digital reputation through behavior you can't possibly control.

POWERING THE METAVERSE

The relationship between disruptive technology and high computation tends to be symbiotic in nature and especially for the metaverse, which combines several of these technologies including AI, VR, AR, and the blockchain. Specifically, virtual worlds require enterprise hardware to create and operate artificial environments and consume an excessive amount of compute power from GPU chips and computer servers.

All these upfront costs add up, especially on the business side. Traditionally, virtual world games needed investors with deep pockets who believed enough in its future to back the project financially for it to even become a reality. Second Life, for example, required over $60 million dollars before it opened its closed beta test program.

On average, the cost to develop and launch an AAA (a term for video games developed by a major publisher with a huge budget for development and marketing) runs between $60-80 million dollars, including a team of 150-250 people, and 2-3 years of development time.

However, both the costs and the time to market are rapidly coming down with the release of new hardware and game engine software including Unity and Unreal Engine, which can be used to produce high-quality 3D worlds or digital twins based on real physical spaces. Microsoft Flight Simulator, for example, consists of over 2 trillion individually rendered trees, 1.5 billion buildings, and almost every road, hilltop, city, and airport on the globe.

This twin world is made possible because of real-world scans. Rather than build from zero, photo scanning technology allows Microsoft to effectively duplicate the real world.

The Epic Games Quixel camera, meanwhile, can generate environmental MegaScans comprised of tens of billions of pixel-precise triangles. Or, for an investment of $20,000 USD, a company called Leica offers photogrammetric cameras designed to capture the details of entire homes, malls, buildings, and other venues with seamless precision. In summary, these proprietary products are making virtual scenes, including films, games, and metaverse worlds, easier and cheaper to build, while dramatically reducing design overheads.

After designing a virtual world, the next challenge is ensuring the high-bandwidth and low latency needed to sync consumer-facing hardware in the form of VR headsets, smartphones, smartwatches, and other devices such as stationary bicycles and haptic gloves. Low latency networks—which reduce the time needed to transmit from one place to another—are vital for delivering the synchronization of facial and physical movements inside the metaverse. This requires high-bandwidth and low-latency Internet service across the entire world and is a challenge that SpaceX's Starlink satellite and other companies are working diligently to solve. It's still unclear, though, whether satellite Internet will be an effective way to resolve latency issues. It's usually faster to send data over a physical cable as there's physical distance for the data to travel; compared to beaming data into space and then back down to Earth, leading to higher latency.

Another challenge comes on the consumer side with delivering seamless virtual and augmented reality environments. But before we discuss the infrastructure challenges of powering virtual reality and augmented/extended reality, let's first look at the difference between these two technologies.

The difference between the two is one of technology as well as intent. With VR, a person wears a headset with goggles and earphones in order to immerse themselves fully in a false environment. AR meanwhile involves the overlay of information onto our regular perception of the world, such as Google Glass. Both make use of advanced head-mounted displays (HMDs), but unlike VR, there are no physical obstacles blocking out natural light around you while using AR devices.

Some people criticize HMDs for their usage being isolating or anti-social. Some research has also shown that users who wear HMDs in public are viewed as less attractive than those without them. However, it's important to note that this criticism isn't unique to HMDs. Most types of eyewear—goggles, reading glasses, or otherwise—naturally make people look different when seen by others.

In the short term, we can expect augmented reality to become more popular widespread than virtual reality as Pokémon Go has shown. This is partly due to AR's lighter method of interaction (assessable through a smartphone and no large earphones needed) and the fact that it can be used for any type of application—not just games—that we see today on our smartphones or tablets.

The first consumer version of Google Glass was released in 2013 in the form of a limited "Explorer Edition". Other companies have also followed in developing AR glasses such as Sony, which has developed the SmartEyeglass.

While these devices did not live up to initial expectations, we're moving from an information age into a fully immersive age where technology will gradually become more integrated into daily life. This includes both AR headsets like Google Glass and VR headsets like the Oculus Rift. The prospect of virtual and augmented reality is an exciting one, as they have the potential to completely revolutionize how we access information and interact with content online. Negative perceptions will also start to change as specialized equipment like headsets and motion trackers become progressively cheaper and miniaturized.

One other challenge facing augmented reality is that unlike, virtual reality, AR requires the correct camera input in order to create a composite image. This means that light sources must be present in order for AR to work (such as light from street lamps or sunlight), and any shadows cast by these objects must also accurately reflect what's seen through the device. This isn't an issue when using VR technology, which can use projected images instead of real-time camera input.

One of the other critical properties is remote presence technology—a very realistic form of video conferencing that can be implemented today using cameras and microphones alongside panoramic visual displays. Virtual worlds using this technology have been around for decades in one form or another, from the early Multi-User Dungeons (MUDs) to graphical games like "The Realm Online" and current MMORPGs (massively multiplayer online role-playing game) such as "World of Warcraft". But the biggest hurdle preventing an open metaverse is the lack of a standard interface.

Currently, most virtual environments are developed under proprietary systems, so that users who move between them must learn new interfaces each time they transfer their presence into a different type of world. Thus, to push this idea into mainstream use, it will take the creation of an open-source system or body of standards by a company or organization.

It's important to note that even if we do get a standard interface in place, one problem will be people's natural resistance to change. Users may not want to abandon the virtual world they already have for various reasons, whether it's based on an old standard or because they've built up a large number of friends there over time. We already see this with chat tools like IRC chat, which have dedicated followings despite being largely superseded by newer online tools for social interaction.

One possible way around this problem would be to keep both types of worlds around simultaneously and allow users to choose—similar to what we see today in Second Life where users can log into either the old Linden Lab grid or the new open-source grid known as "OpenSim." Few projects are pursuing this idea at this point but it's an interesting idea that may help solve the problem of transitions if it were to be put into practice.

The ability for users to access their digital assets and records across all metaverse worlds is also critical to user adoption and the long-term success of a vibrant virtual world. In traditional gaming, users accumulate rewards, a global ranking, and other assets in one game but then start at zero as soon as they decide to enter a new game. However, in an open ecosystem like the metaverse, users' achievements, badges, skins, non-fungible tokens (NFTs), and other assets could be carried over to other worlds, just as kids like to wear merchandise purchased at Disneyland outside the theme park's borders.

While not widely discussed, allowing interoperability between virtual worlds and games can have serious implications on equal opportunity and in-world economics. As each virtual space functions as its own local community, "insiders" might not take kindly to "outsiders" arriving pre-equipped with assets they themselves had to earn within that world as a native user. Allowing outside visitors to bring their virtual assets might lead to a virtual world equivalent of the types of resentment we see directed at tourists, expats, and immigrants in the real world. This may even compel virtual world communities to instate and set rules for new entrants, which could result in virtual passports, virtual import taxes, and even virtual border control analogous to the real world.

Implementing this type of interoperability is also an uphill battle in terms of permission and technology. On the infrastructure side, the sharing of information needs to be done in a way that is repeatable, and understandable between different providers and systems. While this is not easy to execute, Epic Games offers an inspiring precedent in the gaming world.

Part of the success of Fortnite, developed by Epic Games, came from the struggle to overcome traditional anti-competitive practices by being compatible across devices and operating systems. Rather than locking the user experience into one console version, the game can be played fluidly across consoles. This interoperable model means that players can access digital assets, rankings, and reputation accumulated across different versions of the game, such as PlayStation, Nintendo, and Microsoft, which has helped to unlock a larger number of users as well as massive global interest.

Next, on the permission side, individual worlds, including centralized projects like Facebook Horizon Worlds or Fortnite, have to be willing to cooperate with other virtual worlds in the metaverse and approve interoperability, which has few existing use cases in the gaming and entertainment industry (outside of expensive license agreements between game developers and external brands such as Disney and Lego). Even between decentralized platforms, it's currently cumbersome or impossible to transfer assets, skins, NFTs, and in-game currencies from one platform to another.

However, as mentioned, users will still want a single place to access everything they own. To overcome this barrier, VC investor Matthew Balls suggests an additional on-layer metaverse service in the form of a wallet or storage locker that would overcome the need to connect every platform directly. Each platform would simply need to ensure its compatibility with a specific wallet or storage service.

Social channels, including Discord (an instant messaging and communication platform), and secondary marketplaces are also predicted to have a role to play. Discord, for example, has grown to over 250 million gamers after solving the problem of limited communication tools to stream popular games like Fortnite and League of Legends. As a social communication layer, Discord embeds interconnections with different game franchises in an open environment. Secondary marketplaces like OpenSea (a peer-to-peer marketplace for buying and selling virtual assets on the blockchain) also integrate with different decentralized worlds to port the transfer of assets as part of an external ownership layer. While users can't typically transfer native assets from one world to another, it's possible that OpenSea might be used to import non-native NFTs (that don't belong to one particular world), such as digital artwork, from one world to another.

Another partial solution in the domain of interoperability is the Metakey project, which offers a multi-purpose non-fungible token (NFT) that can be used across multiple platforms. Users who buy this token can use it as a special key to transform into avatars, claim game items and exclusive game perks in different worlds, access learning resources on a video course database called Metakademy, access virtual land and events, as well as activate discounts.

Beyond the barriers of interoperability across virtual worlds, there is also the challenge of technology adoption, which has been much maligned throughout the history of AR and VR. In fact, many decentralized worlds are still accessed through a traditional 2D web browser interface without using either of these technologies. Adding AR or VR to recent innovations in virtual ownership, including non-fungible tokens, cryptocurrency, and virtual land, increases the barriers to adoption and limits the number of early adopters. In sum, by requiring users to adopt VR or AR technology to explore their virtual world, the creators are asking the user to not only adopt the idea of virtual ownership and virtual land but also invest in a non-mainstream technology in the form of VR or AR.

The Virtual World Quadrant by James Burke in "The Open Metaverse OS_"
published by Outlier Ventures

Indeed, there is already a proxy contest underway, fought indirectly by the founders of virtual worlds. The division boils down to a technical and philosophical question of whether the metaverse should be "lo-fi" or "hi-fi."

Jamie Burke of Outlier Ventures describes hi-fi as projects that deliberately push the technical boundaries of the experience through software and hardware, such as Somnium Space. Lo-fi, meanwhile, describes projects that design for the lowest possible device and bandwidth requirements for universal accessibility like Cryptovoxels. Other projects such as Decentraland and Second Life straddle the hi-fi and lo-fi battle line and deviate on the other main axis, which is "open" or "closed" in terms of ownership and governance.

INTRODUCTION TO THE
VIRTUAL ECONOMY

For almost every major market in history, being early has been an incredible and unmatched opportunity. By being early, you not only capitalize on early deals and emerging business models at lower cost and with few competitors to speak of, but you're also prepared and well-resourced for future opportunities as the market matures. (The only catch is that the new market must flourish!)

When it comes to building an alternative version of reality for work and leisure, the opportunities and potential of the metaverse are truly unlimited. Perhaps the biggest boundary to innovation is how far you can search into the depths of your own creativity and imagination.

For businesses, the metaverse will offer a number of obvious opportunities. This includes the capacity to communicate more effectively and increase awareness by providing customers with additional information about products and services in a rich and engaging environment or create unique and memorable campaigns. Imagine walking around in a virtual shopping mall and instead of the world-famous Nike logo, you see a giant shoe that you can climb up and jump into, with the actual storefront directly inside. This is just one example of how the metaverse can be used in marketing campaigns to give companies new opportunities to engage with their consumers.

To further understand future opportunities and business models in the metaverse, we first need to examine the basic tenets of a functioning virtual economy. A virtual economy refers to micro-economies within virtual spaces such as online games where participants earn money by selling goods and services to each other.

Each participant agrees to abide by the rules of the virtual economy such that everyone can fairly benefit from it. Aspects that participants typically agree upon are: what can be owned and sold, what can be bought and how much of it, on what terms these goods and services are traded (for example, free trade or restrictions such as first-come first-serve), and whether taxes will be collected on all or some transactions. Business models within the economy are also typically based upon the fact that residents own virtual property or carry out a task in an online game for which they receive income.

One of the most established virtual economies is Second Life, where residents buy land, on which they can build their own business premises or apartments and rent them to other residents. In the game WorldZ, where there is no physical property, residents instead earn money by completing tasks given to them by companies looking to hire agents, and in Entropia Universe, players mine a virtual resource and sell it to the game's developers for cash.

In a virtual economy, the total amount of money is generally derived from two sources: transaction fees paid by buyers and sellers at the time of each transaction (if there are any), and earnings received from selling products or services and through other activities such as owning land or resources. For example, Second Life collects a 10% fee on all transactions between residents but this does not include renting apartments, which is free. Hence, in total, 95% of transactions take place without being taxed (amounting to $100 million per year) yet Second Life has earned more than $200 million since its launch in 2004. Earnings also have their own sources such as rent income obtained by landowners, interest from loans charged within the game, and sales of products created by residents.

Parts of the Virtual Economy

In order to better understand how money circulates in a virtual economic setting, let's now examine the various value components.

Currency

As the connective tissue linking businesses and consumers, currency serves as a vital medium of exchange in the virtual economy—much as it does in the real world.

In a virtual economy, currency is exchanged by users when they buy or sell virtual goods and services, which may also include a small transaction fee. In Second Life, for instance, given that transactions are made using Linden Dollars, there's a charge for a percentage of each transaction. This stems from the fact that Second Life created the currency, maintains its value, and regulates its supply to prevent inflation.

Interestingly, virtual games and platforms have a history of devising their own virtual currency. For fictional worlds not set in reality, such as those set in Space, it makes sense to issue a new currency, but even games set in the real world, such as Grand Theft Auto, prefer to incorporate their own unique currency.

Part of this legacy is to encourage in-game transactions—as players tend not to value artificial currency as highly as real currency (even though real money was used to purchase the in-game currency) and to keep funds locked into the game and not withdrawn and spent in the real world or in other games.

Observing the use of centralized currencies by gaming platforms like Fortnite and Roblox, and the use of cryptocurrencies in decentralized worlds like Somnium Space and The Sandbox, we're unlikely to see traditional currencies including the US Dollar and Chinese Yuan used in the metaverse as a medium of exchange—especially given the fast adoption of cryptocurrencies.

Cryptocurrency can be defined as a digital asset designed to work as a medium of exchange using cryptography to secure transactions and to control the creation of additional units. Cryptocurrencies used in the metaverse, however, have a somewhat different purpose from that of other cryptocurrencies such as Bitcoin, which is primarily used as a store of value and investment.

The primary role of a cryptocurrency in the metaverse is to facilitate commerce and create user-generated content within a specific world (i.e. assets, skins, textures, etc.) in a stable manner. Just as countries prefer to offer their own local currencies (with the notable exclusion of many European countries), virtual worlds such as Decentraland and Axie Infinity can better insulate their economies from external risks emanating from outside their digital borders by using their own native cryptocurrency. The offering of a local currency is also a business strategy to raise capital funds, attract attention, and serve as a vehicle to reward early participants through local currency appreciation against fiat or other cryptocurrencies.

In most blockchain-based worlds, users can buy land or other assets using a native cryptocurrency such as MANA (in Decentraland), CUBES (in Somnium Space), AXS (in Axie Infinity), and SAND (in The Sandbox). The virtual world Cryptovoxels, meanwhile, has switched from its own native coin to the more general-use cryptocurrency Ether (ETH), which is linked to the Ethereum blockchain.

Understanding the many dimensions of the Ethereum blockchain takes dedicated study, but in a nutshell, Ether is a transactional token that facilitates operations on the Ethereum network. This means that all of the programs and services connected to the Ethereum network and in need of the network's computing power to execute are paid in Ether.

We will analyze the Ethereum blockchain in the next section, but for now, it's important to remember that Ether is a cryptocurrency whereas Ethereum refers to the blockchain network supporting applications including non-fungible tokens and decentralized autonomous organizations (DAOs). This means that assets such as virtual land are often purchased or sold in exchange for cryptocurrencies, including MANA and Ether, while the transfer in ownership is recorded on a public blockchain, such as Ethereum and Solana.

Ownership

To build a burgeoning virtual economy, trust and guarantees of ownership are necessary for encouraging participants to spend money, enter business deals, and make large purchases. Traditionally, ownership of virtual assets and virtual currencies has been overseen by central entities in the form of game developers.

In Second Life, ownership of Linden dollars and in-game assets are audited and managed by the game developers Linden Lab. While game developers are properly incentivized to behave fairly and maintain trust over ownership to keep gamers playing, they're not incentivized to allow gamers to take their assets to other platforms. Moreover, game asset rules might be susceptible to change, such as a change in ownership or leadership at the company level. In the past, asset owners have filed class-action lawsuits against Second Life for changing their terms of service that led to the loss of their virtual property.

Second Life users have also encountered inventory loss problems in which a user's paid-for assets temporarily or permanently disappear without warning or enter a state where they no longer appear when requested. This can occur for a variety of reasons, including technical problems and hacks, and with Linden Lab under no obligation to compensate users for lost items. In other cases, Second Life users have reported the failure of other users to honor land rental agreements—much like bad actors in the real world.

Ownership in decentralized worlds, meanwhile, is typically recorded on the Ethereum blockchain, a decentralized, automated, and immutable blockchain ledger that acts as a database for timestamping and recording all of the worlds' transactions.

Before examining the Ethereum blockchain, let's first unpack the decentralized and immutable qualities of a blockchain ledger (for readers new to blockchain technology). Firstly, the blockchain is decentralized as there is no central place for information to be stored. Instead, information is stored on a network of computers, also known as *nodes*. Each of the individual nodes hosts one copy of the blockchain's transactions which removes a single point of failure and removes the threat of corruption from a central authoritative actor.

The blockchain ledger is also immutable in that it cannot be altered and changed. Immutability is achieved because each block of information, including transaction details, employs a cryptographic method to keep the data unaltered. To learn more about how blockchains work, you can check out "A Complete Visual Walkthrough into How Blockchains Work" with Anders Brownworth on the Real Vision Crypto YouTube channel. Let's now return to examining the Ethereum blockchain.

Unlike Bitcoin, which acts primarily as an exchange of value with more narrow usage applications, Ethereum is designed as a general-purpose programmable blockchain used for running a myriad of different program applications, including smart contracts, DApps[8] (decentralized applications), and tokens.[9] Importantly, Ethereum helps to keep track of changes in ownership via tokens.

Derived from the Old English term tācen (meaning sign or symbol), a token is a special-purpose store of value, such as a laundry, arcade, or transportation token. In the offline world, tokens typically represent items of low value and limited application, such as laundry tokens.

Nowadays, tokens have expanded to include digital ownership on the blockchain. Tokens are used to represent ownership of assets, currency, voting rights, access rights (i.e. to a discussion forum or website), and more. These tokens can also be traded or even broken into fragments to transfer the attached asset value, such as transferring a digital art piece from one person to another via transferring ownership of the token. The change of ownership is recorded on the public blockchain to ensure there is no doubt over who owns what.

Tokens can be programmed to serve many functions and can even possess overlapping functions. Similar to how a driver's license might serve both as a qualification and as an identity document, a token can concurrently serve as proof of ownership over a virtual asset (i.e. land) and as a right to vote in that same virtual world.

Tokens are also non-fungible, which means that one token is not directly interchangeable with any other. This means that a digital collectible such as a CryptoPunks artwork tied to one token is not equal in value to a token linked to another artists' artwork. Money, meanwhile is fungible, in that I can fairly trade my one $1 bill for your $1 bill (as these two stores of value are directly interchangeable). Similarly, one Bitcoin is interchangeable with another single Bitcoin, making it fungible.

As with traditional art, non-fungible tokens hold value under the structure of several factors: proof of scarcity (the number of items in existence), proof of creation (who made that piece), and proof of ownership (who currently owns it). Hence, to make a token non-fungible, it must have unique information, including a unique identifier, the number of other identical tokens in existence, and the original creator, which in turn can be tied to the current token owner.

In effect, the creation of NFTs now enables art and other unique assets to be recorded forever on the blockchain in full public view and maintained across many end-points (clusters of computer servers bound to each other using cryptography) around the world that support the underlying blockchain and thereby remove any single-point-of-value.

Later, if the same asset is sold or transferred, this information is again recorded on the same blockchain in the form of a transaction to confirm the current owner of the asset. One can still copy the file of a particular digital art piece but that item has no significant value as anyone can see that person is not the true owner of the original version based on public records (transaction history) stored on the blockchain, which can be viewed at https://etherscan.io/.

What's more, because tokens are programmable, the creators of NFTs can generate revenue on subsequent resales of their tokens. As an example, I recently purchased a SuperWorld piece of land for 0.05 Ether on the secondary market OpenSea, and as the creators of this token, SuperWorld received 5% of the sale price, while the remaining 95% was distributed to the seller (92.5%) and to OpenSea (2.5%) for providing the marketplace for this transaction.

In sum, this system of public ownership over unique assets recorded on the blockchain is revolutionary and lays the path for digital property rights. The fact that NFTs cannot be duplicated and counterfeited on-demand, and permanent ownership is guaranteed, helps to explain the recent interest and excitement over digital assets in virtual games and other digital ecosystems.

Another feature of the blockchain is that it builds trust and removes counterparty risk during the process of transferring digital ownership. Counterparty risk is the risk of the opposing party in a deal or transaction failing to meet their pre-agreed obligations. Traditionally, to avoid this problem, an intermediary was brought into the transaction to ensure both sides cooperated by taking custody and then releasing the exchanged assets to each side following their initial cooperation. This arrangement, while generally secure, introduces another form of counterparty risk in the form of the intermediary failing to execute their obligations or acting in an unfair and untransparent manner.

Contracts coded on-chain, known as smart contracts, effectively replace the need for an intermediary by transferring assets over the blockchain. Rather than using a third-party to oversee the transaction or agreement, a smart contract agreement is written into lines of code and is automatically executed when predetermined terms and conditions are met.

This effectively removes the need for an escrow system. OpenSea, for example, provides a service for buyers and sellers to conduct business but it does not hold NFTs items under an escrow system. Unlike eBay where transactions are based on buyer and seller reputation, transactions on OpenSea take place using smart contracts. You therefore don't need to trust your counterpart will behave honestly like you do on eBay, nor do you have to trust OpenSea as they never assume ownership of the NFT. Once the transaction has gone through successfully, the purchased NFT will be successfully tied to the buyer's Ethereum wallet address and appear in the profile section of their OpenSea account.

Governance

Aside from smart contracts and non-fungible tokens, the blockchain also facilitates the creation of organizations on the blockchain ledger.

Represented by rules encoded as a computer program, decentralized autonomous organizations, known as DAOs, are transparent organizations controlled by their members and not influenced by one central authority. As the rules are embedded into the code—with no managers needed—this system is intended to create an organization that follows strict rules but without any rulers.

This unbundled structure helps to remove hierarchy and bureaucracy as control is diffused across a broad network of participants whose self-interest is served by following the rules in a transparent environment. This means that no individual or group can edit the rules without others noticing. For any changes to be implemented, all members of the DAO (holding that DAO's token) need to vote. This contrasts with many central organizations where changes are led by a central party, such as a board of directors or steering committee, in a private setting.

A decentralized organization operating on the blockchain provides an attractive proposition for the virtual world, where potentially powerful individuals acting under pseudonyms and digital avatars liaise and interact. DAOs, for example, can implement a voting system and diffuse power and decision-making over policies that determine how the world behaves by allocating tokens to members.

In Decentraland, landowners automatically receive voting rights via their land tokens, which allows them to influence decisions on the future development and daily running of Decentraland, including what kinds of wearable items are allowed, content moderation, as well as land and auction policies. This process of governance differs from how important decisions are made in Second Life or on content platforms such as YouTube and Facebook where decisions directly affecting users are made behind closed doors.

One limitation of DAOs is their effectiveness and efficiency at solving complex matters, given that it takes significant time and effort to define decisions and then for members to be fully informed and to reach a general consensus.

In practice, DAO decision-making tends to work best with narrow and clearly defined decisions such as whether to allow or disallow a certain user name. A proposed ban of the name "Jew-Fucker", for example, was enacted through a DAO vote, whereas the proposed ban of the name "TrumpSucks" was rejected by the DAO's voting members.

Virtual Property

Contrary to popular belief, the concept of virtual or digital real estate is not as novel as most people believe. There's been a marketplace to lease and buy digital real estate since Second Life in 2003 and longstanding opportunities to buy advertising space within video games. The reason that virtual property is suddenly gaining more attention now is due largely to the addition of blockchain technology, which verifies digital ownership.

The blockchain enables users to see what transactions have taken place on a public ledger, including previous purchases and how much total land in a virtual world is available. This prevents game and platform developers from quietly minting new land or manipulating the total supply. All in all, this forces the developers to be accountable and builds trust over ownership among all participants in the economy.

In regards to virtual property rental income, this would come in revenue from renting land, apartments, and other virtual properties within the ecosystem. Like the real world, real estate taxes are usually charged on rental transactions or sales of land, in which developers are charged a small portion of the land sale when they sell them to investors.

In addition, brands are incentivized to lease or purchase land to advertise in the virtual economy. Inspired by the flashing billboards in places likes New York's Times Square, brands will want to advertise near high-traffic plazas or land parcels in order to promote their products, services, and events. This means that virtual real estate developers can charge brands to advertise their products or services within their domain similar to ad-banner slots sold on Google. Alternatively, brands can elect to purchase their own land and build interactive experiences to expand their reach and engage with in-world consumers.

Taxation

In the real world, governments apply taxes to maintain infrastructure (including roads, parks, and libraries), pay for public goods and services, maintain border security, and support citizens in need of assistance, among many other government services.

In the virtual world, though, there are far fewer public overheads. Once a park is minted on the blockchain, there are zero costs to keep the grass looking green and no overhanging branches to trim. Also, part of the attraction of the metaverse for some early adopters is the lack of central government oversight and aggressive tax collection.

Nonetheless, there are still costs to running a virtual economy, including web hosting fees and user experience upgrades, as well as decentralized autonomous organizations and community grants to fund. Logically, a quasi-taxation system that redistributes funds to the platform for public services is still needed for platforms to function and communities to flourish.

Tax collection can be conducted through a form of general transaction tax or another system, which is not particularly difficult but might only be implemented once incomes reach a certain level, something that is solved once the build-out phase is complete.

The obvious target for tax collection is landowners, who are the most likely participants to derive value from commercial activities conducted in the virtual economy. This may mean modest property taxes paid by landowners (who lease their land) to the platform but could also be collected from services that take place on their virtual property, such as digital art sales.

To help maintain equalized demand and supply for land through taxes, virtual worlds in the metaverse might also need to charge a small portion of the total sum collected from real estate properties sold in their world.

Jobs

Jobs are a pivotal component for growing a virtual economy, but until recently, jobs have also posed a barrier to the growth of virtual economies such as Second Life, Minecraft, and Roblox.

While there are certainly avenues to earn income and gain partial employment in these and other virtual games, the ability to earn a living has been limited to a small percentage of users. As a consequence, if the majority of individuals are not employed in the virtual world, then these users spend less time there as they are obliged to seek employment in the physical world, which between travel and work, consumes a large percentage of their waking hours. Without work, users can't earn money to pay for activities and digital goods in their virtual leisure time.

For the virtual economy, job scarcity puts a cap on virtual earning potential and consumer spending, which in turn translates to flat economic growth. This structural glitch in the virtual economic system, though, is beginning to dissolve in light of the COVID-19 pandemic. According to the forecasting company L'Atelier, the global virtual economy is currently worth over $100 billion a year and employs hundreds of thousands of people in online jobs.

While virtual labor has existed for most of the 2000s prior to COVID-19, jobs performed on websites such as Upwork, Amazon MTurk, Fiverr, and TaskRabbit, tended to be menial, repetitive, and low cost. Now, with recent changes to practices in the workplace and the coming technology underwritten by web3, the traditional micro-tasks of the virtual economy are becoming increasingly complemented with more advanced and complex job roles. At present, technology allows many workers to work from home and forego the need to work in an office environment. While such jobs are delivered virtually, the output of this labor contributes largely to the real-world economy.

In its current form, Facebook[10] and Twitter's public embrace of virtual work does very little to drive the growth of the virtual economy in worlds like Decentraland, Somnium Space, The Sandbox, and Cryptovoxels. However, this trendline towards off-site work lends currency to the future of collaboration and co-working in these virtual worlds.

Eventually, rather than ask employees to collaborate over Zoom and voice calls, employees will be expected to attend meetings and other work activities using an avatar in a virtual office in the metaverse. Not only will this help to drive adoption of the metaverse by coercing people to spend more time there, but it will also increase the growth of the metaverse economy through spending on virtual office leasing, construction and architecture, digital avatars and fashion, and other virtual items and services.

As an important footnote, the 8-hour day is unlikely to be directly converted to the virtual world where your boss's avatar can look over your shoulder and monitor your whereabouts—especially given the physical fatigue of wearing a head-mounted device. Instead, virtual offices in the metaverse will provide a second workplace for interactive activities such as meetings, training, and collaborative work that employees sign in and out of over the course of the day (while still working at home or offsite).

Competition

For an economy to grow and prosper over the long term, competition is a proven and highly effective market mechanism. Competition encourages entrepreneurial spirit and economic expansion as entities compete to bolster productivity, promote innovation, improve quality, and reduce costs.

In the case of the metaverse, competition is needed to ensure that there's a multitude of experiences and worlds rather than one single dominant world. According to Tim Sweeney, the CEO of Epic Games, "If one central company gains control of this, they will become more powerful than any government, and be a god on Earth" (in reference to the metaverse). If Facebook, for example, owned the entire metaverse, then the virtual economy would simply be less open and less attractive—a single dominant company would act in its own interests, in ways that would tend to limit the powers of smaller developers and individual users.

Similar to the development of the Internet, the metaverse's virtual economy will thrive from independent developers and artists are who are incentivized by the opportunity to sell their products and services and to fill gaps left in the market by larger players.

Beyond building an open and competitive economy, competition is also needed in other realms of the global economy including real estate, jobs, and governance through decentralized organizations.

WHO WILL FILL THE
METAVERSE?

As an additional layer of the Internet with no single destination, the metaverse will be filled with many virtual worlds, each offering unique virtual experiences.

In terms of what the first true metaverse domains will be, there are a number of prominent contenders. Graphical virtual environments such as Decentraland and Somnium Space, voxel-based worlds like Cryptovoxels and The Sandbox, as well as VR games including Axie Infinity are well-posed to continue gaining in popularity. Each of these worlds will be introduced and critiqued later in this chapter.

Some might also say that Second Life, the massively multiplayer online role-playing world launched in 2003, already fulfills much of the technical criteria for powering a true metaverse world. Second Life has a large and multifaceted economy and a sizeable user base who actively create content and trade virtual goods. Second Life also supports a large number of concurrent users (averaging 40,000 or so at one time). This alternative world, however, remains heavily centralized, closed, and controlled by Linden Lab, who are the developers of Second Life. The ability of the developers to remove users, access any information, change the rules of the world, and print more money can negatively impact asset ownership, trust, and long-term decision-making, which therefore makes Second Life more reminiscent of Web 2.0 than web3.

Another major contender is Facebook (now renamed Meta) and CEO Mark Zuckerberg has a lot planned for Oculus, the virtual reality company he acquired in 2014. By building out a metaverse world, Facebook wants to enable its users to further explore online social networking through unique 3D environments. This is part of Facebook's planned transition from a social media company to a metaverse company, with over 10,000 employees in the company already involved in building consumer hardware including AR glasses and other metaverse projects.

Facebook's vision is to create the computing platform after mobile—where people can build completely new experiences and make VR available at scale. By creating this virtual world, called Horizon Worlds, Facebook users will be able to communicate with friends, family members, or colleagues from all over the world, anytime and anywhere.

Within Horizon Worlds, users can explore virtual worlds as they grow and develop while discovering all sorts of new things that interest and inspire them. This includes playing games, meeting people from all over the world, solving puzzles together, trading virtual goods, or creating digital spaces. Development of the world will also be boosted by a USD $10 million creative community fund for supporting community competitions, an accelerator program, and selected developers.

Creations in Horizon Worlds can range from designing 3D objects with a set of shapes and tools, all the way to developing elaborate multiplayer games and interactive experiences using visual scripting. Community members can also resize themselves to work at different scales, so they can make themselves small enough to work on tiny details or large enough to enjoy a full view of their work.

In addition to Horizon Worlds, Facebook has released a Horizon Workrooms app for users to work remotely in VR, which allows users to work together in the same virtual room, regardless of physical location. Combining features including mixed-reality desk and keyboard tracking, hand tracking, remote desktop streaming, video conferencing integration, spatial audio, Oculus Avatars, and the Oculus Quest 2, users can join a meeting in VR as an avatar or dial into the virtual room from their computer via video call. Horizon Workrooms is available free to download on Oculus Quest 2 in countries where Quest 2 is supported.

In sum, the emphasis of Facebook's virtual world is on virtual reality and social interaction—without some of the decentralized virtual economy features mentioned in the previous chapter. Facebook's massive user base and ownership of Oculus, though, remain important ingredients for building a mainstream VR-first social world.

As mentioned, Facebook isn't the only player racing to fill the metaverse slipstream. In terms of other emerging metaverse projects, Decentraland, Somnium Space, Cryptovoxels, The Sandbox, SuperWorld, and Axie Infinity are also close to the forefront of industry innovation and new user adoption.

Let's now take a look at each of these virtual worlds in closer detail.

Decentraland

Founded in Beijing by Ari Meilich (Project Lead) and Esteban Ordano (Technical Lead), Decentraland is the most established and well-known of the decentralized virtual land projects. Beginning in 2015, the founders created a proof-of-concept for recording ownership of virtual real estate on a 2D grid of pixels using blockchain technology. This provided the blueprints for developing Decentraland, which was released as a 3D world to BETA users in 2017, before opening to the public in February 2019.

The Decentraland world consists of three layers. The first layer is the consensus layer, which uses an Ethereum smart contract as a ledger for managing asset ownership. This layer also contains a description file, which is how each landowner tells the platform what they want to serve at their respective land location(s). The next layer is the content distribution layer, which is a decentralized system of storage that Decentraland uses to distribute content needed to create its virtual world. The third layer is the real-time layer, which allows users to communicate with one another via a peer-to-peer connection.

The Decentraland world is also divided into parcels of land designated by x and y coordinates on a two-dimensional map, similar to how towns and cities are partitioned in the real world. The Decentraland map consists of privately owned parcels of land (16 by 16 meters in size and limited to 90,000 parcels) and public land that cannot be bought or sold, such as roads, and plazas owned and controlled by the platform.

Roads are marked in grey on Decentraland's in-game map and private land is marked in blue. If the land parcel is available for sale, it will show as light blue on the map. Other large plots of land have been set aside for plazas, which are owned by the Decentraland community, marked in green on the map.

Each plaza has its own theme. The most central plaza on the map is called the Genesis Block Plaza, which acts as the starting point for all avatars entering Decentraland. The Decentraland developers also released a Content Creator Program in May 2021 that adds new features including the ability to teleport to a friend's location, issue friend requests, and encrypted in-game chat.

Content Building

As an owner of a private land parcel, you have complete control over its design and appearance, with no interference from Decentraland's development team (aside from a potential policy violation). Parcel owners can create content on their land using the Decentraland Builder or the Decentraland SDK (software development kit), which is a developer tool that allows you to create by writing code.

Similar to click-and-drag building tools found in The Sims game franchise, you don't need any advanced technical knowledge to build and modify content using the Decentraland Builder. However, there are some limits to what you can create using this tool. To create applications, games, videos, outbound links, buttons, avatar modifiers, and 3D scenes, you will need to use the Decentraland SDK.

After installing the Decentraland SDK, you can compile and preview your scene locally inside your chosen command-line interface tool. In Decentraland lingo, a scene is an experience built on top of one or multiple parcels of land. While players can walk freely from one scene to the other, the code for each scene is sandboxed from other external scenes. This means that elements contained in one scene won't cross over into a scene on someone else's parcel as each scene exists as its own miniature self-contained world. Sound generated in one parcel, for example, can only be heard by players positioned inside that parcel. (Note that visitors can turn off sound in their user settings.)

In terms of video scenes, there are currently two methods to display a video in a scene. One method is to stream the video from an external source by referencing a URL or video file path. The second method is to store the video file within the scene as a .mp4, .ogg, or .webm file. However, keep in mind, there's a memory limit of up to 15MB per parcel. Storing a video file on your land will therefore contribute to the total size of your scene and this will make the scene slower to render when visitors enter your world. You can, though, minimize video size by compressing the original video file.

After testing the scene locally, content can be uploaded directly to your land in Decentraland. To learn more, see the Decentraland SDK 101 guide (https://docs.decentraland.org/

development-guide/SDK-101/) or search the tags **decentra-land** or **decentraland-ecs** on Stack Overflow.

Trading Land & Other Assets

Land parcels can be traded peer-to-peer at market value over the blockchain, allowing people to buy or sell land to other users on both the Decentraland Marketplace and the secondary market OpenSea.

Normally, the closer a land parcel is to the Genesis Block Plaza (the world's starting point), the higher its market value. Other factors that might impact the price of the land parcel include proximity to a major road, district, or another plaza.

Aside from land, users can buy and sell wearables and names for their avatars on the Decentraland Marketplace (also available as an app inside the Samsung Blockchain Wallet) or external marketplaces including OpenSea. These items exist as NFTs recorded on the Ethereum blockchain and can be bought or sold using Decentraland's MANA token, which functions as Decentraland's in-game currency.

MANA

MANA can be purchased on most major cryptocurrency exchanges, including Coinbase, Gemini, Kraken, and Binance. MANA itself is an Ethereum ERC20 token and has a finite supply, including a built-in mechanism to burn (permanently reduce) total supply over time. Originally, the burn rate was 2.5% per transaction. However, this protocol has since been changed, with a new 2% levy on Decentraland Marketplace transaction fees redirected to community projects via the Decentraland DAO.

DAO

The Decentraland DAO is a community-based mechanism for decision-making in this virtual world. Holders of the MANA token are eligible to vote on issuing grants, important changes to Decentraland such as building height limits and token economics, as well as day-to-day operations, including content moderation. Users receive 1 vote for each unit of MANA they own on the Ethereum address they use to vote. Owners of private land in Decentraland also receive 2,000 votes per parcel they hold and owners of estates receive 2,000 votes per parcel of land in each estate. This therefore gives landowners—who have a higher financial stake—greater input on the future direction and day-to-day running of Decentraland.

As a community-based mechanism, decisions take time, dialogue, and social momentum in order for proposals to be formed, voted upon, and implemented. Examples of proposals already passed include the ability to sit on chairs and point at things, as well as a lost land retrieval proposal (that mimics existing laws in the real world). This feature makes it possible for lost or abandoned land to re-enter the real estate market after a set period of inactivity.

It's important to remember that the Decentraland DAO does not have full control over Decentraland. The DAO, for example, does not own the MANA smart contract, which was destroyed upon deployment.[11] This avoids any individual or consortium gaining permission to modify or pause the total supply of MANA.

Visiting Decentraland

Anyone can visit Decentraland and traverse the map, however, only landowners (or users leasing land) have the ability to create and monetize content hosted on their land.

To visit and explore Decentraland, you will first need to sign up for a free account and customize your own avatar, including sex, facial features, and hair color using the Avatar Editor, which also includes a limited selection of free wearables and accessories. If you want to customize your fashion later, you can purchase digital leather jackets and other wearables from the Decentraland Marketplace using MANA or earn them by participating in different events.

To receive or spend MANA, you will need a browser extension wallet, which at the time of writing is the MetaMask (meta-mask.io) browser wallet. After installing MetaMask as a browser extension (be very careful to install the official version of Meta-Mask and not a phony version), you will be able to log in to Decentraland. Note that you don't need to have any MANA in your digital wallet in order to explore, spend time, and attend events inside Decentraland. However, if you wish to buy MANA using fiat (i.e. USD, Yen) or another cryptocurrency (i.e. Bitcoin), you will first need to purchase MANA on an exchange such as Coinbase and then transfer the funds to your MetaMask wallet. You cannot buy cryptocurrencies directly using your MetaMask wallet. After you have transferred funds to your wallet, you will be able to make in-world purchases in Decentraland.

Events

In regards to events, Decentraland hosts a broad spectrum of virtual activities including conferences, music concerts, art showings, community meetups, pride parades, and even digital dog shows.

In April 2020, Decentraland hosted the Blockdown Crypto Conference, which was attended virtually by crypto entrepreneurs Erik Voorhees and Roger Ver, Binance CEO and Founder Changpeng Zhao, and music artist Akon.

While fanfare around the event was flat, Decentraland also hosted the first Crypto World Cup for football, with the winners receiving an NFT that could be redeemed for actual gold in the real world.

Why You Should Pay Attention

While Decentraland still struggles from a somewhat clunky user experience and a modest number of daily active users, the land market on the platform has been developing rapidly on the back of speculation and finite supply. This in turn has helped to attract media coverage and interest in the platform—also aided by Decentraland's early entrance to the metaverse ecosystem.

Decentraland lags behind other platforms in regards to VR integration and user stickiness. However, it still remains a preferred option for commercial partnerships, major events, and brand promotions courtesy of its powerful SDK tool, which makes it possible to create sophisticated virtual events, concerts, and in-world experiences.

To learn more about Decentraland, you can join their Discord (information on their website) and create a free user account that will allow you to explore Decentraland from your web browser.

The Sandbox

Developed originally by Pixowl (acquired by Animoca Brands in 2018), an established gaming company headquartered in Argentina, The Sandbox appeals strongly to gamers and is one of the most promising user-generated content (UGC) projects in the evolving metaverse.

Before launching a decentralized version of the game in 2018, Pixowl developed mobile-first virtual worlds for iOS and Android called The Sandbox (2011) and The Sandbox Evolution (2016)—competing directly with Minecraft and Roblox in the user-generated content genre. Since the original release of The Sandbox in 2011, Pixowl has focused on creating an immersive platform where players can create virtual worlds and games.

Their recent transition (under the ownership of Hong Kong-based Animoca Brands) from a centralized UGC game to a decentralized UGC game now rewards creators with ownership of their creations in the form of non-fungible tokens. Moreover, the blockchain version of the game allows players to have input as well as partial control over the direction of the game through a decentralized autonomous organization—without a central authority calling all the shots.[12]

By turning traditional centralized gaming on its head, The Sandbox not only hopes to attract users interested in decentralized gaming projects but to also convert players from traditional gaming and disrupt the dominance of Minecraft and Roblox in the user-generated content market.

Content Creation

Like the Minecraft and Roblox franchises, The Sandbox world is a voxel-based environment. Voxels are 3D square pixels—similar to building blocks—that can be edited and manipulated to quickly create objects and virtual world environments.

Players can build in The Sandbox using a free tool called VoxEdit, which is a simple-to-use 3D voxel modeling tool and NFT creation package. The tool allows players to create and animate 3D objects including humans, animals, vehicles, foliage, tools, and other virtual items. At the time of writing, the VoxEdit tool is compatible with both PC and the Mac.

Created objects can then be exported from VoxEdit into The Sandbox Marketplace as an NFT game ASSET, which can be traded and purchased by other players. The object's metadata, including the creator and issue number, as well as transfers of ownership, are recorded publicly on the Ethereum blockchain. ASSETS also possess different levels of rarity (Basic, Rare, Epic, and Legendary) that impact their value, with scarcer items typically attracting a higher valuation.

In addition to VoxEdit, there is The Sandbox Game Maker, which can be downloaded and used to quickly build free 3D games using no-code visual scripting tools.

Tokens

Several token types exist in The Sandbox to connect players, creators, and landowners, and carry out the smooth running of its virtual economy. The basis for all transactions is SAND[13], which can be purchased on cryptocurrency exchanges including Binance and Gemini. The maximum supply of SAND is 3 billion tokens, but the current circulating supply is well under 1 billion, which means that more tokens will be released in the future.

The other two game tokens are ASSETS, which is a token allocated to players who create and assemble user-generated content, and LAND, which is a unique digital piece of real estate recorded on the Ethereum blockchain. LAND is capped to a total supply of 166,464 pieces, which interconnect to form The Sandbox map. Each LAND parcel is 96 meters by 96 meters (roughly an acre) in size and can be populated with games, assets, and other interactive content experiences. LAND, as with other in-world assets, can be purchased using SAND.

Multiple adjacent LANDS are known as an ESTATE, and can be used to create and host larger online experiences. Districts can also be formed to create unique regions of the map but must fulfill certain criteria. For example, the district's LAND parcels must be adjacent, owned by a minimum of two players, and are subject to community approval via a voting system.

Notable landowners in the Sandbox include Snoop Dogg, Atari, The Walking Dead, and the Bored Ape Yacht Club art project, which has driven up land prices for plots adjacent to these landowners.

DAO

SAND also plays a secondary role in the form of voting rights via a decentralized autonomous organization called the Foundation whose role is to support The Sandbox ecosystem. The Foundation funds and incentivizes high-quality interactive content and game production on the platform through a grant program for creators.

These grants are partly funded by a fee capture model with a 5% levy on all SAND token transactions. The SAND collected via this levy is split evenly (50:50) between the Foundation and what is called a Staking Pool (which provides passive revenues on staked[14] LANDS in the form of SAND).

Users that own SAND can exercise voting rights on key decisions in The Sandbox, including Foundation grants to content and game creators as well as feature prioritization on the platform's product roadmap.

Why You Should Pay Attention

From the graphics to the in-world features, The Sandbox performs highly in terms of gamification and aesthetics, reflecting the creator's roots in game development. The ability to build a high-quality single or multi-player game experience on virtual land has the potential to draw in aspiring game developers and gamers to engage in the platform for entertainment and development purposes rather than solely for speculative and commercial motives.

The slow but gradual rollout of land releases also has the potential to attract more people to become involved in the project. As a voxel-based world, The Sandbox is likely to become increasingly popular among Roblox and Minecraft fans, especially among Gen Z gamers. The Sandbox website and associated software tools are also available in Chinese, Japanese, and Korean, which is rare among English-language metaverse projects and shows potential for growth in Asia.

Somnium Space

Starting in 2017 and launched in 2018, Somnium Space is a 3D world where users are encouraged to explore and engage via VR equipment. This includes Oculus, HTC VIVE, HP, VALVE, all Windows Mixed Reality headsets, and other major headsets. In late 2021, Somnium Space also unveiled plans for developing its own standalone VR headset.

Like Decentraland, ownership in Somnium Space is recorded on the Ethereum blockchain and transactions take place in a local currency called CUBES.

Somnium Space is intended to operate independently as if it were an island nation in real life, hosting its own economy and history. In addition, users can earn and accumulate Karma, which represents their social status or how others perceive them. Karma levels are calculated based on a combination of factors including how other players rate them (weighted based on the Karma of the other players), total playtime, world discovery rate, land ownership, building activity, organizing events, and many other behavior-based factors. This system of social status in Somnium Space is not found in most other decentralized worlds and helps to encourage an active community.

In fact, users have gone to great lengths to create the Somnium Times (https://somniumtimes.com/), a user-generated publication with regular news posts about activities in their virtual world.[15]

Somnium Space's German founder, Artur Sychov, is also highly active, spending 2-4 hours each day in Somnium Space, including attending virtual events and spreading his vision on podcasts and through YouTube interviews. Sychov, it's worth noting, is a former investment banker, MBA graduate, and a father of three children. He, much like other metaverse creators, owns properties in his metaverse but still has to pay for land and assets like everyone else.

Sychov is also not alone and works with a team of ten plus employees that help him with building out the Somnium Space world. The Gemini Frontier Fund, a venture fund founded by the Winklevoss twins is also invested in the Somnium Space, with Tyler and Cameron Winklevoss participating as official Advisors to the project.

Content Creation

As with other worlds introduced in this chapter, users can buy land or rent virtual homes, create, import, and trade NFTs with the goal of creating experiences on their virtual land.

There isn't a finite supply of land parcels in Somnium Space, with new plots dropped based on actual user demand. This means the supply of land is not as scarce as Decentraland or The Sandbox and prices are generally lower in comparison.

Land can be used to showcase 2D or 3D art, open a storefront, or host other experiences. Game developers, for example, can host game demos or entire games on their land and live-streamers can host their virtual studio within Somnium Space.

After purchasing land on the platform's Marketplace or a secondary market like OpenSea, you can download the Builder to your computer. This is a click-and-drag software tool used for building and uploading VR structures to the Somnium Space world. The Builder comes with a high level of customization including many modular building elements and colors options.

Each parcel of land is allocated a number of building credits (set according to the size of the plot), which can be redeemed to buy elements such as a window or a door. Installing a single wall, for example, will cost two credits and will be automatically updated on the on-screen credit meter.

Once built, all users can walk onto your land and play games or enjoy other experiences by inserting the local currency CUBES (without necessarily paying gas fees for the experience[16]). Gas fees serve as a transaction fee that users pay to Ethereum blockchain miners to have their transactions recorded and included in the next block.

Somnium Space is a scriptable world, which means that you can program and monetize virtual scenes on your land (including animation, video, and body movement tracking) and create digital assets too. This includes full-body avatars, cars, and world tokens (NFTs that can be placed on land), which you can upload and sell on their Marketplace. This is all made possible using the Somnium UnitySDK, but this option is orientated towards more advanced creators with programming expertise.

Somnium Space also offers a fully programmatic VR advertisement plugin that can be used to capture and analyze engagement, gaze tracking, and conversion rates.

Lastly, it's important to note that Somnium Space actively protects children from adult content such as gambling and discos. Somnium Space follows an opt-in approach to user and age verification. For instance, when you upload content to your parcel, it is automatically flagged as an 18+ parcel by default, and users who haven't completed age verification will be unable to see and experience what is constructed on that parcel. All users, though, can roam the virtual world without needing to complete age verification.

Why You Should Pay Attention

Somnium Space is an early leader in VR integration and potentially in hardware as well, rivaled only by Facebook Horizon Worlds, and offers a social karma score that encourages in-world activity. Its community is robust and certainly an asset in encouraging others to adopt VR technology and join Somnium Space. Among other decentralized user-generated worlds explored in this chapter, Somnium Space is slightly less talked about, with wider user adoption maybe restricted by the need for consumer hardware to enjoy the full virtual reality experience.

Somnium Space is also yet to launch a DAO to enact community decisions and the future direction of the platform appears heavily reliant on its talented but lone founder.

Cryptovoxels

Cryptovoxels is a decentralized, virtual reality, and voxel-based world. The project was unveiled in black and white in 2017 by its

Founder Ben Nolan (who previously worked on the initial build-out of Decentraland as a web developer) but is now available in full color.

As with other virtual worlds built on the blockchain, virtual land is considered a non-fungible digital asset where each piece has its own ID and state and is recorded on the Ethereum blockchain. This allows for full ownership of your creations in this virtual world, which is different from other voxel games such as Minecraft and Roblox where you only have usage rights but no actual ownership stakes. Additionally, as voxel data is stored on the blockchain, records of your creations will not be completely lost even if the virtual world is shut down in the future.

Similar to Somnium Space, Cryptovoxels is compatible with the Oculus Quest, Oculus Rift, and HTC Vive. To find the latest compatible WebVR browser, you can also check out webvr.info.

Content Creation

The main focus of Cryptovoxels is for users and developers to build on the platform, whether that be an MMO, a game with quests, or to simply make more buildings. The world consists of its founding city called Origin City and newer islands, which have streets owned by The Corporation, and parcels purchased and owned by individuals. Owners of these parcels can add and remove voxels (blocks) and features on their parcels or assign their land as a sandbox parcel, allowing other users to build on the parcel for free. In addition, you can practice building on a free editable space off the grid (findable under your account settings).

Coding skills aren't required to build, as voxels can be put in place using the click of a mouse, but building or editing can only take place through a web browser.

Cryptovoxels also offers a scripting interface that lets you run javascript code on your own server and send updates to your scripted Cryptovoxels' parcel. You can write scripts inside any feature on a parcel and everyone that enters your land sees the same scripted view.

Token

Cryptovoxels previously used the SCOLR token as its in-world currency, which could also be used to add color blocks to the world. The token was discontinued in 2020 through a buyback scheme. At present, Cryptovoxels uses Ether for in-world transactions, including land purchases.

Land can be purchased as NFTs on OpenSea and imported using a compatible wallet such as MetaMask and the Coinbase Wallet. New land is dropped on a weekly basis.

Why You Should Pay Attention

While some people are initially resistant to voxel worlds (including myself who didn't grow up playing Minecraft or Roblox), Cryptovoxels is extremely interesting to wander around. The platform also has a slightly old-school feel, both in terms of design aesthetics and the fact you can find random easter eggs in Origin City, which appeals to long-time gamers, and helps to attract a highly enthusiastic (and some might say cult-like) following.

On the development side, Cryptovoxels is similar to Somnium Space in that it offers VR integration and has an active founder (in Ben Nolan), who pays special attention to communicating changes and bug fixes on Twitter as well as encouraging creativity and helping artists to grow their presence on the platform.

SuperWorld

Launched in 2021 and inspired heavily by Pokémon Go, SuperWorld is a decentralized and augmented reality (AR) platform layered on top of Planet Earth. Users can claim one or more virtual plots of land, which are geographically mapped to the real world, including football stadiums, historical monuments, or even your local block.

In total, there are 64 billion virtual plots of land in existence. Each plot measures 100m x 100m, which is approximately the size of a New York City block. As unique NFTs recorded on the Ethereum blockchain, these scarce plots of land can be collected and traded by anyone with a digital wallet and the necessary funds to invest. New plots can be claimed and purchased for 0.1 ETH on the SuperWorld website, alongside gas fees for using the Ethereum network. Claimed plots of land can also be purchased on secondary marketplaces including OpenSea, where plots can sell for many multiples greater than the original price.

As a landowner, you can curate the experience on your plot by creating AR games, interactive 3D art and objects, video, display advertising, and more, which is viewable using augmented reality via the SuperWorld smartphone app, similar to the Pokémon Go mobile game.

Why You Should Pay Attention

The familiarity of layering this metaverse world over locations in the real world makes SuperWorld an attractive option for NFT buyers, especially for those with a sentimental connection to real-world locations. The platform, however, remains new and the ability to generate significant revenue (outside of buying and flipping properties on secondary markets) is not well known or tested. Overall, there is great potential for SuperWorld or a similar decentralized platform to attract massive popularity by capitalizing on the earlier success of Pokémon Go in the AR and geo-location genre.

Axie Infinity

Developed by the Vietnamese studio Sky Mavis, Axie Infinity is a decentralized game marketed as "play-to-earn", with gameplay strongly reminiscent of Pokémon.

The game has already exceeded 1 million daily users and is a global leader in decentralized gaming. Mass interest in the game was driven by viral adoption, especially in the Philippines. This mass adoption began in May 2021 after Yield Guild Games posted a YouTube video showing Filipinos in Cabanatuan City earning a healthy income from the game. Within a week of its posting, the story was picked up by VentureBeat, CNBC, and Hypebeast, and a number of local Filipino news sites.

The game also has high-profile backing including an investment from Mark Cuban, the owner of the Dallas Mavericks and a featured investor on the TV show *Shark Tank*.

What makes Axie Infinity unique from traditional gaming worlds is the blockchain economics used to reward players for their contributions to the ecosystem. This gives users the benefit of permanent and independent ownership of their in-game assets. Instead of locking asset and currency ownership inside the game, players have the ability to sell their assets for in-game currency (the AXS token), which can be withdrawn and converted to fiat currency.

Axie Infinity also elegantly layers its blockchain features behind a compelling and fun game with the same gameplay loops that bring people back to traditional games. Conversely, games that put blockchain technology first and gameplay second are at risk of high player churn.

Gameplay

The game takes place in a virtual world called Lunacia and is filled with little creatures called Axies. Players can collect, trade and even breed Axies as well as battle them to win prizes. The Axie creatures in the game are NFTs, and Axies spawned through the game's breeding mechanics are recorded as a unique NFT on the Ethereum blockchain.

The game is part of a greater ecosystem where all participants are rewarded for adding value to it, which takes place through three main channels.

1. **Axe Battles:** Game players need a team of three Axies—each possessing different skills—to battle against computer-controlled opponents or other real-life players. Each Axie has its own axe, which they level up by battling with other players' axes. These battles are automated so there is no grinding. Players earn rewards by winning battles.

   Player against player battles take place on Ethereum smart contracts. When a battle begins, two players bid an amount they'd like to bet (the maximum bet is 10% of their current balance). If both parties agree, the contract automatically executes when the auction ends at a pre-defined block height or if one of them backs out before then. Every participant gets rewarded based on their winning percentage and contribution.

2. **Breeding Axies:** By playing and battling, players earn resources that can be used to breed new Axie NFTs, which can be later used for battle or traded for tokens. The breeding mechanism allows players to breed two of their Axies together to create an "egg", which can inherit three types of genes[17] based on its parents.

3. **Land:** The Axie homeland, Lunacia, is also divided into tokenized plots of land. These plots provide the homes for players' Axies and can be upgraded over time using a variety of resources earned from playing the game. Landowners can also find tokens on their land plots or task their Axies to explore resources found on other parts of the map.

Why You Should Pay Attention

Axie Infinity became the number one Ethereum game in 2021 and has achieved spectacular success on the back of network effects and its play-to-earn system. While the adoption of other decentralized platforms has been led by speculative interest in virtual real estate, Axie Infinity has proven that gameplay is a faster way to populate a virtual world with active users and foster a prospering virtual economy. The fact the game is compatible with Android phones, the iPhone, and the PC, also makes it easier for everyone to participate.

Upland

To round out this chapter, it's worth briefly mentioning Upland. This blockchain game is an important case study as it offers insight into the risk of media hype and other red flags to avoid as an investor.

Similar to SuperWorld, Upland's players can buy, collect, sell and trade virtual property based on real-world addresses. The world map, though, is a graphical representation and not compatible with augmented and virtual reality hardware. Players' land ownership is recorded on the blockchain and rewards can be earned for completing tasks issued in the form of Upland's in-game currency uPlexa (UPX).

The game received notable press in early 2021 but player interest and UPX token value have since fallen flat. Despite significant user acquisition conducted via paid marketing channels and media coverage, the project has struggled to hold onto users. Part of the problem is the inability of the game developers to ship promised feature updates listed on their website, but the bigger issue appears to be a lack of community and general incentives to play.

While media coverage and paid advertising are proven methods for acquiring traditional gamers, virtual world and user-generated content games require a strong and active community to add value and attract new users, which offsets the absence of traditional game mechanics in the form of levels, battles, gripping narratives, and overall game progression.

Part of the reason Axie Infinity went viral was the fact that users were deriving significant economic value from playing and this encouraged others to join and for entrepreneurs to create commercial endeavors inside the game. This organic activity naturally attracts other users to participate and helps to build a strong virtual economy.

To close this chapter, it's important to note that while some of the projects discussed in this book are current leaders in the race to build the metaverse, there is no guarantee that they will continue to grow and survive in the future. As with earlier phases of the Internet, new contenders will replace legacy players, just as Google overtook Yahoo and Ask Jeeves in online search. Even so, there may be more opportunities for a multitude of players in the metaverse to exist—as compared to the winner-takes-all stakes of Web 2.0.

NETWORK THEORY

Network theory is a popular lens in the blockchain industry and has many working applications to understanding the growth of the metaverse.

As an interesting and powerful theory for understanding many different systems, ranging from biological organisms to Facebook social connections, network effects have already been fundamental to user adoption of web3 projects including cryptocurrencies, NFTs, DiFi (decentralized finance), and metaverse worlds.

Network theory typically refers to graphs with nodes and edges. A project or a community is represented by the graph, with nodes in the graph depicting individual users or other subjects and edges illustrating ties between those nodes. Nodes have "rank" based on how central they are to their respective networks while also having tie strength or weight, which is determined by size/diameter. A key challenge with many projects is determining who are the key nodes or influencers involved. This task is not simple but can be achieved using software tools like Cytoscape and Gephi.

The edges, meanwhile, determine the number of connections each person has to one another. If the graph has only one node, then there are no edges, and the network is essentially worth nothing. Facebook, for example, doesn't work well with only one user and no edge connections. If you add a second node, then the network is valuable if you want to connect with the first node via the edge joining those two nodes. Now you can communicate directly with Mark Zuckerberg from his dorm room at Harvard. However, if half the world is connected to that original node or the various other nodes, then suddenly the network becomes one of the most valuable networks on the planet.

Once a network becomes popular following an increase in the number of nodes and edges, you can start to build products and services on top of the network, such as Facebook mini-games. The more people that are connected, the more likely the network is to create value. The value of the network can also grow exponentially as more nodes are added. This is known as Metcalfe's Law, and it suggests that you should value a network based not only on its number of nodes or people but also the number of connections they have with each other.

If Facebook gains more users, for example, then it will gain more value either through increased demand for friends to connect with or through increased utility. These self-reinforcing loops are very difficult to break once they gain market momentum.

Another example of this type of network can be seen on crypto websites such as coinmarketcap.com. This website ranks and tracks all the various cryptocurrencies and provides information such as price, market cap, and volume. This information is valuable because it allows you to see which projects are gaining traction (market value) so that you can decide whether or not they might be worth investing in or using for other purposes. The website generates revenue from advertising, but, this is only possible if blockchain projects have grown their user base to the point where there is significant traffic on the CoinMarketCap site. In other words, without network effects there wouldn't be a thriving crypto community surrounding these types of websites, which gives them their inherent value.

When it comes to assessing the potential value of metaverse projects, we can look at how affiliation networks impact the growth or decay of these projects. We can do this by looking at how people are spreading information regarding individual metaverse projects via social media sites such as Twitter and Reddit. We can also look at people creating YouTube videos, writing articles, participating in Discord chat groups, or recording podcasts about specific metaverses. All of these mediums can be categorized as affiliation networks or referral systems because they are providing outside traffic and awareness to the metaverse ecosystem (in addition to the users that are already there).

Affiliation networks impact the growth of a project through viral marketing, which allows these platforms to quickly build out large user communities. However, it's very important for projects to think about retention post-viral marketing so they don't lose all of their early adopters if something causes members in the community to stop transacting with each other, as experienced by the Upland virtual land game.

The next important aspect of network theory is threshold effects, which is where there is a big difference between small and medium-sized networks and large ones. In other words, it's easy for two or three people to be connected but once there are groups of more than 10 or so participants, the dynamics begin to change as larger groups become increasingly difficult to manage especially when you can't guarantee that every person will work together given individual objectives. This is why blockchain technology as a whole meets inherent limitations when looking at it strictly through the lens of network theory.

The blockchain by definition is a network where everyone follows the same rules/protocols. The problem is that most people aren't incentivized to follow those rules unless it's in their best interest to do so. This will not always be the case but without some leeway with regards to how participants can interact on a platform, you inevitably run into problems because humans are complex creatures who don't necessarily do what they're told. However, blockchain technology does have some positive use cases in the form of voting, supply chain management, and storage of records/ownership, which are areas where trust and disintermediation provide value for both businesses and individuals.

Network effects also have a potential disadvantage in the form of "free-riding", where people take advantage of a product without paying for it. This problem occurs on open-source platforms because some participants don't contribute to the code base but still take advantage of using it for free.[18] This is analogous to a company that doesn't employ any employees and just profits from selling products without paying taxes.

In terms of the metaverse, it's important that users are creating value in the metaverse through business model development, community-based decision-making, and, of course, social interactions. User-generated worlds require a large amount of content creation from a variety of creators in order to build value and attract more users to the platform. If ownership of most properties is owned by professional investors—too busy in the real world to explore the virtual world—and those properties are left vacant as a passive investment vehicle, then this creates few incentives for new users to spend time in that world and contribute to the greater economy and ecosystem.

As we can see, network effects play an important role in the growth of virtual communities and project development because they allow platforms to increase demand/utility by growing their user base and providing inspiration and value in the form of affiliate networks pushing traffic to those ecosystems. It's also hard to build a metaverse world without incentives diffused equally throughout the network, which is why new virtual worlds that come online are likely to give away virtual land at rock-bottom prices in order to encourage adoption and community growth—as other projects before them have done.

It's crucial to repeat at this point that network effects and affiliate networks only allow these virtual worlds to grow communities if they actually have an underlying experience or service that people need. If a virtual world doesn't have something valuable then it's impossible for its affiliate networks to gain much traction because their audience has no way of knowing about the project and thus won't be incentivized to promote it.

Consequently, the most important takeaway from this chapter is that metaverse adoption relies strongly on underlying user value, which in turn relies on network effects and affiliate systems as tools for growth. To this end, we can expect virtual gaming worlds such as Axie Infinity—with its broadly diffused incentive system—to be greater catalysts for widespread adoption than say Decentraland where there is a cap on the number of users who can benefit from owning virtual land.

Adoption in the Global South

As discussed, in order for a trend to grow, there needs to be incentives diffused throughout the network to incentivize more people to participate, share, and contribute. In advanced economies, the average citizen is often resistant towards the concept of alternative worlds because they value the in-person relationships, locations, and experiences already available to them, labeled as "reality privilege" by some observers.

Moreover, convincing someone to change their mind and lead their peers to think differently is tantamount to asking that person to change tribes and nobody wants to modify their worldview if loneliness is the outcome.

The narrative, however, is somewhat different in the global south (a term used to describe the regions of Latin America,

Asia, Africa, and Oceania, which are more likely to be low-income and politically or culturally marginalized in the global economy), where for some people, an alternative world offers more opportunities, new experiences, and a more vibrant environment than their own world.

At the time of writing, there are leagues of gamers earning USD $500 in tokens per month playing Axie Infinity. This is a life-changing source of income for these gamers. In 2021, approximately 50% of the one million daily active users are living in the Philippines.[19] The metaverse therefore has great potential for adoption in countries like the Philippines, which can be accessed by any individual with a mobile phone and a reasonable Internet connection.

Blockchain gaming communities are also finding innovative ways to engage and reward users with shortages of available upfront capital. To play Axie Infinity, mobile gamers need to invest well over USD $1,000 to build a starter team of Axies to play the game. To overcome this barrier to entry, an informal market has emerged where existing owners of Axies can lend their digital assets to other gamers in exchange for a percentage of their potential winnings, with earnings typically split 60:40, 50:50, or 70:30.

This scheme, often referred to as a "scholarship", allows Axie owners (who typically own more Axies than they have time to manage) to increase utilization and returns from their digital assets, and helps bring more new users into the game while facilitating the transfer of knowledge and skills between new and experienced players. To maximize earnings, the owners of Axie teams are incentivized to provide tips and share knowledge with their scholars, including best combos and how to farm resources efficiently. In addition, scholars have a direct line of communication with veterans of the game to troubleshoot technology-related questions such as managing a crypto wallet or how to cash out their tokens.

As an unofficial service in the game, matching currently takes place outside the game client and dashboard through direct relationships (such as co-workers, relatives, Facebook, Twitter, Reddit, YouTube, or Discord contacts) or, more commonly, through entrepreneurial-minded guilds who buy and loan out their assets or provide a third-party matching service. Yield Guild Games, for example, pairs players with assets owners using a Uber-like matching system.

Metaverse projects also have the potential of reducing other barriers through VR technology. To provide an example of how virtual worlds can be used for this purpose, we may see actual city landmarks replicated or replaced with virtual copies to allow people from around the world to visit major cities without having to travel there. This means that developing countries will be able to create virtual cities that could increase tourism revenue from visitors who can't afford physical travel, with tourism being one of the top three industries within many developing countries, thereby providing jobs such as local tour guides as well as economic benefits.

In addition, virtual worlds could be used to improve real-world business operations by allowing businesses to create virtual copies of their products or services and show how they work before the physical product is even made. Such a solution would be helpful in connecting a country's economy with existing markets by providing virtual replicas of products, reducing upfront costs, as well as showing potential customers what products look like or how they work without having to send a physical prototype.

In many countries, the metaverse is expected to help improve current online learning systems through the use of avatars, which would allow students to attend lectures without physically being there. In China, for example, there are rudimentary plans to develop a metaverse in order to help China's rural population access

information online and to leverage experienced and knowledge-
able teachers in a more scalable manner.

BUSINESS MODELS IN THE METAVERSE

The Internet gave birth to many new services we didn't have before and these services have accumulated to give us what we call the second Internet era or Web 2.0. These services include social media networks, e-commerce, music streaming services such as Spotify and Pandora, crowdfunding platforms, live-streaming, and much more.

However, with virtual reality gradually on the rise and more VR headsets being pre-ordered by consumers than ever before, it's no surprise that entrepreneurs are looking to jump on a new emerging market. According to a Zion Market Research report, the global augmented and virtual reality market is expected to grow to approximately USD 814.7 billion by 2025, far above its value in 2018 of 26.7 billion before the COVID-19 outbreak.

The metaverse is still in its infancy but for those who act quickly and are patient to wait for the industry to mature, there any many lucrative business opportunities awaiting. Sooner or later, almost everything that's possible in real life is likely to be replicated in the metaverse, in addition to new services and business models built on web3 technologies.

No one can predict what's going to happen in the metaverse once it turns mainstream. For now, we can only speculate on what new business models are likely to emerge from here. Each person has their own prediction, based on previous experiences with similar technologies, but, ultimately, we do know it's going to be huge. So let's have a look at some of those business models already available and under development today.

Virtual Goods

The trade of virtual goods is one of the more established business opportunities already thriving in the evolving metaverse. Untethered from supply chain shortages, shipping costs, concerns over ethical and sustainable practices, and the laws of physics (i.e. gravity), virtual goods offer high margins and a massive potential market.

Virtual goods include digital clothing, shoes, accessories, weapons, furniture, appliances, and other objects that only exist in the virtual world. Virtual face masks, for example, were sold as wearables in Decentraland back in 2020 as part of a partnership with Binance to raise funds for fighting the pandemic. Second Life, meanwhile, has featured well over 2 million virtual items on its online marketplace.

Brand activation for well-known luxury and consumer brands is already underway with Gucci opening a store in Roblox called Gucci Garden. One digital Gucci bag sold, for example, sold for USD $4,000 on Roblox in 2021. Other brands, including Adidas, are also following suit with expansion into the metaverse and virtual goods.

In the future, brands venturing into digital fashion are expected to become more innovative and intelligent in designing items for wear in the metaverse. Italian luxury fashion label Off-White's founder, Virgil Abloh, says he wants "to make virtual clothes to paint pictures physical clothes cannot, and let buyers access a new dimension of their personal style – no matter who they are, where they live, and the virtual worlds they love".

Virtual Malls

While online shopping is usually an activity done alone, this is about to change with the spread of virtual stores and malls. Shoppers will be able to shop for virtual clothes, visit their favorite brands, and peruse virtual art alongside friends from around the globe, all in one location.

Compared to the physical world, shoppers will be able to visit dozens of storefronts in dramatically less time and with less friction. One hypothesis holds that consumers will act more aware and responsive during the shopping experience without the friction of queues, closing hours, renting a trolley, finding a bathroom, staff shortages, and many other obstacles encountered in the real world.

One of the early contenders in the virtual retail space is Redfox Labs (www.redfoxlabs.io), which hopes to drive the adoption of virtual retail shopping in Southeast Asia. Consisting of 120 shopfronts (each created as their own NFT), Redfox Labs is opening a mall called Virtual Space where participating brands can purchase or lease a shopfront from other participants, including the ability to rent storefronts by the hour or for a designated promotion period.

Digital Art

For digital artists, the metaverse offers an ideal platform to showcase art in a 3D space and reach interested and cashed-up buyers. Artists can open their own virtual gallery in all the major worlds, including Decentraland and Cryptovoxels, where avatars can buy, browse, and even talk directly to the artists via voice chat.

In addition, the metaverse provides artists a platform to build a community and host digital events. This is one of the reasons why the popular Bored Ape Yacht Club NFT art project is making investments to acquire land and host events inside decentralized platforms. This includes building their own club on land purchased in The Sandbox, with admission reserved for those holding a Bored Ape NFT in their MetaMask wallet, similar to the exclusive Black Sun club depicted in the novel Snow Crash.

The world's oldest auction house, Sotheby's, has also built a digital replica of their London New Bond Street Galleries in Decentraland's Voltaire Art District.

Commenting at its opening in 2021, Michael Bouhanna the Specialist and Head of Sales at Sotheby's said, "We see spaces like Decentraland as the next frontier for digital art where artists, collectors and viewers alike can engage with one another from anywhere in the world and showcase art that is fundamentally scarce and unique, but accessible to anyone for viewing."

Online-to-offline & E-commerce

In the web3 era of the Internet, many of the e-commerce websites we know and love today are likely to have a virtual presence in the 3D world—replacing part of today's reliance on 2D images and online catalogues of products sold on e-commerce websites.

Businesses, including food outlets, will increasingly look to adopt an online-to-offline (O2O) model by creating a presence in the metaverse. Dominos Pizza, for example, has opened a small kiosk outlet in Decentraland where users located in the U.S. can order pizzas at their kiosk and then enjoy food delivered directly to their physical address.

At the same time, brands can leverage the many benefits of traditional online commerce by running an unmanned storefront 24 hours a day without traditional cost overheads such as coat hangers and mannequins. Dresses and other items can simply levitate in metaverse outlets, unconfined by gravity.

Customers, meanwhile, can try on clothes and see items inside an immersive 3D rendered environment as part of a new buyer experience that starts in the metaverse and connects with the real world. After trying on and paying for products in the meta-verse, consumers can receive their purchased items via the mail in the real world.

The ability to try on clothes in a virtual setting is also expected to reduce returned purchases (due to poor size fitting) and reduce the negative effect that returned items cause on the environment (i.e. wasted and non-recycled packaging, transport-related carbon emissions, and the destroying of returned items purchased via e-commerce). In the U.S. alone, up to 30% of all online purchases are returned with return shipping generating over 15 million met-ric tons of carbon dioxide emissions each year (equivalent to the emissions from 3 million cars).[20]

Virtual Real Estate Development

Virtual real estate, as discussed in the previous chapter, has enormous commercial potential in the metaverse. Similar to web-site domains, virtual land will serve as the digital ground for virtual malls, retail strips, casinos, and many other lucrative metaverse business models.

For virtual real estate developers, there is an incentive and commercial benefit of owning interconnecting plots of land called estates or districts. This is not just to lock up valuable parts of the map but to create unique value and implement a shared vi-sion.

By owning plots of land adjacent to each other, developers can create districts founded around a shared interest or common theme and then drive targeted users to their coordinates on the map. Entertainment districts, for example, might be populated with VR movie theatres, games, social meetups, music concerts, and other live performances. In regards to sport, a designated district might offer a place to play digital sports or watch sport taking place in the real world, such as the FIFA World Cup, with venues from the real world having a digital twin in the metaverse. There may also be special neighborhoods dedicated to a specific team, league, or sport, and public venues for engaging and socializing around that common interest, including sports clubs and official outlets showcasing a team's jersey and other digital merchandise.

Examples of districts found inside Decentraland include Dragon City and China City (which promote Chinese culture, architecture, and social activities), SportsFanZone, Fashion Street, Vegas City, Amusement Park, University, and Museum. These unique districts allow visitors to discover and access relevant content and experiences quickly, while also building a high-traffic and valuable asset for district developers and land owners.

In each world, aspiring virtual real estate moguls typically compete to acquire large land assets for reserving and forming future districts—sometimes even before these worlds become open to the public. This includes individuals who've never owned physical land like Anshe Chung and professional real estate companies and traditional investors from the real world.

In Decentraland, the leading real estate developer and investor is Republic Realm, which made headlines in 2021 for land purchases valued at USD $900,000.[21] By receiving capital from credited individual investors in the real world, Republic Realm allows investors to participate in price appreciations and profits generated from investing and managing digital real estate, including inside Decentraland.

Republic Realm's flagship asset in Decentraland is a virtual shopping strip called Metajuku, inspired by Tokyo's Harajuku shopping district. In Metajuku, avatars in Decentraland can buy digital products, skins, and other virtual goods. Republic Realm's other premier investment in Decentraland is a collection of private islands sold as NFTs that give people the Richard Branson experience of owning a private island, complete with access to an exclusive beach club limited to those NFT owners.

With their investment in Decentraland and other metaverse platforms, Republic Realm is hoping to profit on the creation of new virtual brands and the growth of existing crypto native brands, including DressX[22], that will dominate in the new era of the Internet. As a quick sidenote, Republic Realm also runs a series of online courses about the metaverse and NFTs under their Republic Realm Academy.

Another major and notable landowner in Decentraland is DCL Blogger or Matty, who started flipping land in 2017 and eventually quit his job to focus full-time on trading in the Decentraland real estate market.

Similarly, in Second Life, Anshe Chung famously became the first real-world millionaire in Second Life after converting her initial investment of USD $9.95 by flipping and renting virtual real estate over the course of 2.5 years.

Decentralized Gaming

Online gaming is already a massive and lucrative market and many traditional games including The Sandbox and Roblox have transformed or are in the process of transitioning to a decentralized game model.

Other gaming platforms are blockchain-native, including Star Atlas (staratlas.com), which is a massively multiplayer online (MMO) game built on the Solana blockchain. With real-time graphics using Unreal Engine, Star Atlas already offers cinematic-quality video game visuals and is gaining a strong user base.

The main focus of this section, though, is on small game developers. Similar to how Zinga Games achieved success by releasing application-based games on Facebook (including Farmville), new game developers will be able to build a franchise and gain exposure by launching on a decentralized platform like The Sandbox, Netvrk, Decentraland, or Gala Games.

Specifically, game developers will be able to purchase or lease land within these decentralized worlds and create a gaming experience compatible with the underlying platform. Game developers, therefore, will need to weigh up the costs and benefits of launching their game on a specific platform, including the content creation tools, cost of buying/leasing land, and the availability of land in a game district or suitable location.

Graphics too will be an important consideration, especially given that decentralized worlds such as Decentraland lag traditional games in this department. Graphics on decentralized platforms, however, will continue to improve as new and existing platforms take advantage of new powerful hardware, which is needed for displaying images closer to reality and rendering high-quality special effects for multiple active concurrent users.

Developers will also need to consider how to best tailor their games to a given platform's user base as well as the ability to earn revenue from those players. With that in mind, revenue will mostly come in the form of micro-transactions, which is the ability for game developers to charge a small fee to play or to purchase items within the game. This is an obvious way to make money and follows a proven business model.

Gambling

Gambling has already established an early foothold in the virtual world through blockchain casinos and horse betting games.

Blockchain casinos are similar to online gambling websites except that the winnings are paid out in cryptocurrency (and not fiat) and punters partly own the casino by owning the tokens/

cryptocurrency of that casino as a form of equity and which also allows them to be involved in both governance and decision-making.

One of the more prominent projects in this space is Decentral Games (https://decentral.games), which is the first community-owned metaverse casino. Players pay to gamble and take their winnings in the local $DG token. By holding $DG tokens, the players also effectively own the casino through membership in the $DG DAO. This means that players holding $DG tokens can vote and decide on what new games to add as well as other new features proposed for community voting.

Other virtual casinos can be found within many of the decentralized land-based worlds including Decentraland and Somnium Space. Decentraland has its own Vegas District with a number of virtual casinos open to the public, including one venue opened in 2021 by Atari. Users can play a variety of popular casino games including slot machines, Roulette, and Blackjack. Some casinos have even started hiring people (through their digital avatar) as croupiers who work shifts helping to explain tasks to users such as placing a bet or spinning a roulette wheel.

Lastly, horse betting has proven to be hugely popular, as evidenced by the runaway success of Zed Run (https://zed.run/), an NFT-based horse racing game where users can buy, breed, race, and trade digital horses.

It's important to note, however, that gambling activities exist in a grey zone due to the absence of Know Your Customer (KYC) policies within some decentralized worlds.

Decentraland, for example, and its casino owners currently have no KYC verification process to verify a user's age and place of residence. At present, Decentraland notes the following warning on their website's Terms page: "If you reside in a jurisdiction where online gambling is banned (such as the United States of America, China and South Korea) you must refrain from accessing

Content which includes online gambling."[23] They also provide a warning on the same page against minors engaging in gambling activities inside Decentraland.

Gambling services were also mentioned in the Financial Action Task Force's (FATF) 2020 Virtual Assets Red Flag of Money Laundering and Terrorist Financing report, which sighted gambling as a means to launder cryptocurrency, and the need for online gambling services to take appropriate steps to mitigate this risk.

Construction

Given the time-consuming nature of creating elaborate constructions, especially for highly customizable creations such as private islands or casinos, a new jobs economy of virtual architects, voxel designers, and builders is emerging. There are already professional virtual service providers in this space including Voxel Architects, LandVault, and Polygonal Mind, as well as freelancers finding work on Upwork or in Discord chats.

As seen in Second Life, virtual construction ideas may also inspire construction in the real world, with players using 3D printers to recreate buildings from the virtual world in real life.

Education

One of the most interesting applications of virtual and augmented reality is its use for education. Complementing existing massive open online course (MOOC) platforms such as Coursera as well as traditional universities creating virtual institutions as a new mode of delivery, the metaverse will unlock new areas of education by giving students the ability to visualize complex concepts as they relate to the real world. The USDA Forest Service, for instance, has created a smartphone application that allows users to see an overlay of forest boundaries on top of their view of the real world.

Similar examples include overlaying a simulated lava flow to show where an eruption might happen as well as how lava flows interact with other terrain features and using virtual objects to help surgical residents learn faster. For instance, if a patient has certain vital organs that need to be removed during an operation, virtual hints can be used to show the surgeon exactly how these organs are being positioned.

Another new interesting application of education is the capacity to teach empathy through virtual simulation. One example is the film "Notes on Blindness: Into Darkness", which premiered at Sundance in 2016 and has since been adapted into an immersive virtual reality project that takes the user through the sensory and psychological experience of blindness. Through a series of 3D virtual scenes, the metaverse will make it possible to understand the experiences of people from different races, sex, and other categories that would not be possible without the application of a digital avatar within a virtual environment.

Additionally, the metaverse offers a safe place for students who suffer from social anxiety, physical bullying, or who would otherwise experience forms of discrimination in the real world.

Finally, while metaverse-based education is unlikely to fully replace the need for offline in-person education, it will help to close the gap between those who do and those who don't have access to tutors and high-quality education.

Events

While the virtual world might still have a residual reputation for being anti-social, public and private events are already a major selling point of spending time in the metaverse. From art exhibitions to music concerts and after-parties, all the popular virtual worlds are holding regular virtual events.

Moreover, events in the metaverse won't just be partying and flogging digital art. Other formats include educational events such as a startup boot camp where avatars interact in a virtual space to design and ship a product, virtual tours, professional events, conferences, and language learning meetups.

Potential business models here include event management companies, venues-for-hire, emcee and DJ-for-hire services, event marketing, and even virtual wedding planners.

BUYING YOUR FIRST VIRTUAL PROPERTY

While virtual property is an exciting opportunity—with some observers proposing virtual land as the biggest land grab in many decades—it's worth mentioning the elephant in the room and that's the infinite supply of digital land. If virtual land exists on the vast cosmos of the Internet and recorded on a never-ending blockchain ledger, how can virtual land hope to hold value or rival and exceed the value of physical land? This is a big question and an important hedge to swing over before buying your first virtual property.

No different to website domain names, there is, indeed, no hard cap on the supply of virtual land available on the Internet. Some worlds such as Decentraland and The Sandbox can intentionally limit land allotments, which might drive up their market value, but new virtual land will continue to be created in other worlds and especially as market demand increases.

As the CEO of Epic Games, Tim Sweeney, explains "Just as every company a few decades ago created a webpage, and then at some point every company created a Facebook page, I think we're approaching the point where every company will have a real-time live 3D presence, through partnerships with game companies or through games like Fortnite and Minecraft and Roblox."

In order to give everyone an opportunity to participate in the metaverse, more and more virtual land will be created, and similar to the value of website domain names, the specific content and traffic directed to that location is where intrinsic value will be generated. In the fashion of .com, and more recently, .io domain and .xyz names, supply for highly sought-after virtual land will be constrained by numerous factors including their location. Certain worlds, districts, and other central locations land will be more valuable due to their proximity to valuable places such as virtual theme parks, popular game scenes, access to foot traffic, and specific communities.

How Virtual Real Estate Differs From Offline Real Estate

While there are many similarities to investing in physical and virtual land, there are also many differences and, in fact, benefits to buying property in the virtual world. Notwithstanding the obvious benefits of owning property in the real world, especially with having somewhere to power your laptop and having a bed to sleep in, the virtual world is far more versatile and convenient to get around. Some virtual worlds, for example, allow you to teleport. This means that you can type in the coordinates of a location and instantly arrive there. However, in other virtual worlds, you need to journey from a set starting point like you would in the physical world at walking or running speed.

This particular piece of information is vital when it comes to buying land, as you will typically want to maximize proximity to the virtual world's starting point(s), but this may not matter if users can teleport to their destination, which makes the exact location less crucial.

The next major difference is the low overheads. At present, there are no land rates paid to a local council for public services such as garbage collection, no monthly electricity, and no water bills. Also, unlike the real world, there are far fewer unexpected costs that may arise due to a myriad of problems, such as tenant issues, natural disasters, and poor building material quality.

For the large part, there are minimal costs post the purchase of your property aside from potential construction costs. In fact, the biggest obstacle is likely to be the inflation of contractors caused by either wild currency appreciation or growing demand for construction services. In addition, unreliable or unresponsive contractors may cause some delays to construction.

Lastly, it's important to reiterate that virtual land is not a direct substitute for physical land. You definitely cannot store unused physical objects, eat, drink, or live your life exclusively in the metaverse. Even with virtual reality headwear, you still need a roof over your head and a physical address for pizza delivery. Virtual land is simply a destination on the Internet, much like a website domain or a Facebook page.

From another perspective, virtual land is actually a destination within a destination, as its contained within a virtual world (such as Decentraland or Somnium Space) as a single parcel, estate, or district.

Buying Land

As with purchasing real estate in the real world, there are several investment approaches to buying virtual property. The two most popular methods are Buy & Hold (known affectionately in the crypto world as "hodling") and Buy & Flip (or "flipping" for short), which both apply to investing in the metaverse. Let's first explore the difference between these two investment approaches.

Buy & Flip

With the Buy & Flip method, you buy a property and hold on to it for a certain period (usually a short time) and then aim to sell the property at a profit. In other words, instead of buying a property for you to keep, you are purchasing it solely as a short to mid-term investment.

Those who flip properties generally buy distressed real estate properties and then sell them at a profit. In most scenarios, once a house is purchased, the new owner then has to get to work repairing and renovating it. However, this doesn't always have to be the case. Sometimes, the owner may simply want to hold on to the property and find the right buyer or opportunity to resell it.

To arrive at a certain desired profit margin, the buyer needs to take into account their upfront investment, renovation costs (if applicable), and cost of sale (including transaction fees, listing fees, agent commission, and royalties to the developers of the virtual world) with the end goal to buy low and sell high, meaning they sell the property for more than they spent on it. The entire process involves calculated risks and strategies, and when implemented correctly, is an effective and proven path to financial freedom.

In addition to buying low and selling high, buyers are typically aiming to sell the property within the shortest time possible—either within a few months or, at most, a year. However, in the virtual world, it's possible to flip properties in a matter of hours or even minutes, which offers several advantages.

The first advantage is the ability to purchase more or better properties using the profits generated from previous sales. By cashing in on your gains (consisting of property appreciation and even currency appreciation), you can expand your portfolio (either in quantity or quality) of properties in less time. This theory only works if you are arbitraging the market by adding value to your property above the market rate for that type of plot during the flipping period or through superior negotiating and buying skills. For instance, if you sell an empty plot of land for $10,000, following the sale, you can still only buy one equivalent plot of land using that $10,000. However, if you create a business or a new structure on top of your parcel of land to add value and then sell it for $20,000, suddenly you're able to buy two new empty parcels of land valued at the market rate of $10,000.

Secondly, if you are recording profits to generate capital to invest in multiple properties, then you can afford to diversify across multiple virtual worlds. This reduces your reliance on one world, which may experience a market collapse due to user churn or the rise of other competing virtual worlds. At the beginning, you may only have the funds to invest in one property, but through a series of profitable trades, you may be able to afford purchasing two properties in two separate virtual worlds.

Also, while the metaverse and web3 are set to partially replace Web 2.0 infrastructure, there are no guarantees on which metaverse worlds will survive in this new era. Given that, you may want to flip a property or two at a profit while you can or at least diversify your portfolio.

Next, because you are frequently buying and selling multiple properties, you will inevitably develop your purchase or bidding skills, market knowledge, as well as develop a personal network of virtual contractors, architects, voxel designers, professional buyers, and other virtual professionals. This means that you will soon have a network of people you can turn to for help or resources.

Lastly, it sometimes makes sense to profit during a bull market and especially in the NFT space. Cooper Turley, a crypto strategist and manager of a social DAO called Friends With Benefits, explains that "You really need to take profits in this space. I think we are in an unprecedented territory where the amount of money being made on NFTs every day is unlike anything I've seen in my five years in crypto. It is not sustainable, it is extremely addicting, extremely exciting, and it will not last for a long time. So if you are someone who has been fortunate enough to buy NFTs that have gone up 5x or 10x against ETH, please recognize that is an extremely unlikely scenario to happen over a consistent period of time."[24]

Buy & Hold

As mentioned, flipping a property is not the only way to invest in real estate. Another approach that you might like to adopt is the Buy & Hold strategy.

Following the Buy & Hold strategy, investors hold onto a property by renting it out to someone else.[25] Under this method, the mortgage is usually slowly paid off from the monthly rent (or other rental agreement). The long-term plan is to build equity and allow the property's value to appreciate. The time from the purchase of the property to its sale is typically around five years.

While mortgages are common in the real world, most buyers in the virtual world are paying the full amount upfront, especially given that entry-level properties can be acquired for less than 5 figures (USD) in most virtual worlds. (The mortgage industry for virtual land is also not fully established, at least, for the time being.)

Choosing the Right Strategy

When choosing your investment strategy, you'll first need to evaluate your investment goals. If you are planning to create financial gains in the short term, holding properties might not be the right strategy. Flipping properties allows you to make gains in the short term, which you can reinvest into future properties and flip them for even bigger returns.

In a holding strategy, the property value greatly influences your returns. If the value increases slower than the rate of inflation or the project loses buyer interest, then you stand to make a loss. However, if the value outpaces the rate of inflation, then you stand to make a profit on the market.

Lastly, when it comes to devising your property investment strategy, you should keep into account the native currency token. Decentraland and The Sandbox, for example, offer their own in-world currency in the form of MANA and SAND respectively, which can be used to purchase property, pay for contractors, and purchase materials as a form of exchange. However, these worlds are also recorded on the Ethereum blockchain, including smart contracts that dictate who owns which properties as well as voting rights. This means that the value of your property will not only be exposed to the value of that particular in-world currency, but also the underlying blockchain. In other words, when you convert your fiat into MANA to purchase land in Decentraland, you are not only making a bet on Decentraland and its local token, but you are also exposing yourself to the market value of Ethereum in the form of Ether—plus the price of gas fees.

This is why you will often see the rising or falling value of MANA partially tied to Ether. The more investment that goes into Ether (based on functional upgrades to Ethereum and not just speculation or hysteria), the more confident you can feel about owning land recorded on that specific blockchain.

Researching the Market

Before you can even think about buying a virtual property, you will first need to take a close look at the market. Here, there are a few steps to keep in mind during the assessment stage to help you make a decision.

The first step is to research the market. Look at what virtual properties are available in the area of focus by visiting them if you can and reviewing their specifications on secondary marketplaces.

You can find prices available on the official websites of each virtual world or on a secondary marketplace like OpenSea. To follow live updates in the Decentraland property market, you can follow a Decentraland bot on Twitter that pushes live updates of accepted bids/sales for parcels of land (https://twitter.com/dclandbot). For The Sandbox, the Metagamehub DAO[26] offers a free machine learning pricing algorithm tool that projects the expected market value of a given parcel at that given time (https://www.metagamehub.io/valuation).

Whatever digital source you use to find information, you need to find out the average price at which a category of plots are purchased. This may mean creating a spreadsheet consisting of recently sold and for-sale properties of a certain size in a given world and locale.

Taking the sale price of previously sold properties, you can roughly work out a suitable offer price. Let's say that you discover the average sale price of properties is USD $10,000. While you were checking the average price, the lowest price point happened to be USD $8,000. So, you can make an offer at around that price range, and perhaps not above USD $10,000.

Besides recent sales, there are also other considerations to take into account. For instance, in the physical real estate market, experts often advise you to consider the growth in property prices over time. The theory is that a market that shows steady growth means that at whatever price you purchase the property today, there is a high chance of earning a profit in the future.

While this rule of thumb may apply to buying property in the metaverse in the future as the market matures—for the time being, at least—you can expect most virtual properties to go up quickly in value in the short-term but also for major crashes to happen in the short to mid-term as well. As the market is still in its infancy, there is lower buyer conviction on what virtual worlds will survive and which local areas of these worlds will thrive. At the moment, value appreciation is widely driven by speculation and investors are still discovering new virtual business models to plant on their land. Inevitably, there will be volatility and bubble bursts, either in a given world or potentially in the greater metaverse as cryptocurrency prices swing.

Next, you will need to decide whether you want to buy an undeveloped plot of land or move straight into an "end-product", so to speak, such as a boutique island in Decentraland. The decision will be largely decided by how much time you have and your interest in virtual construction.

In addition to narrowing down on the type of property, you also need to decide on the area in which you are going to focus your efforts. Looking at an area with high rental growth might present you with opportunities. But that also means the asking price of the plot will be high. In other words, you will have to invest a lot more to get the land. Typically, rental prices increase when there is rising demand for certain types of properties or areas, such as properties in a gambling or shopping district. This is why buying land near say an Atari plot in The Sandbox or Metajuku in Decentraland may make sense, as these district owners may need to buy or rent plots in the surrounding area in order to expand their district. You may also want to double-check the DAO section of the platform's website for any recent or current votes to create or approve a new district in that world.

While marketplaces will tell you how much the property is valued, you will have more confidence in your plans if you virtually go to visit the property. This is also one more way to check if the NFT listing is genuine or not.

OpenSea, for example, provides a link where you can view the property on a map and which will typically provide an option for you to drop into that position on the map via an avatar. Note, however, that worlds that are yet to officially open (including Treeverse and The Sandbox as of 2021) will not allow you to explore the land via an avatar until their world is publicly released, which limits your chance for reconnaissance.

Once you know what you want to buy, then you can start to find them and view them in their virtual world. When you assess properties, you gain valuable information about them that can help you decide whether you would truly like to invest or not. There are a few things to consider when you start assessing potential properties.

First, you will need to assess what is currently built on the surrounding land and who owns it, as this will also affect the value of your property. Remember too that you will receive any of the content built on the land once ownership is transferred to you.

Next is foot traffic. Is your property located in the virtual wilderness or are there other avatars passing by regularly? This variable is important if you wish to create a business that relies on avatars dropping in and easily locating your property, or for setting up billboards on your land.

However, given the early-stage development of most worlds, don't be alarmed if you only see a handful of avatars or less in the space of an hour. While it's impossible to forecast future user adoption, you can add a multiple of say 5-10 based on user growth in that world. Alternatively, if you see more avatars in one location than in another location, then that is perhaps a more reliable metric to benchmark potential foot traffic. Also, you may need to test different times of the day as avatars will be logging in at different hours based on their geographic location. For example, you might see plenty of North American avatars at 8pm, but few European avatars at that same time point.

At a higher level, you also want to consider the overall level of engagement and retention among users in that world. You can do this by reviewing the number of active contributors in a virtual world's Discord server (there will be a link on their website to join), including the number of people saying "gm" (good morning) on a daily basis. If there's been no meaningful discussion, including no "gm's" for several days at a time, and no evidence of users coordinating Zoom calls to discuss ideas and projects, then maybe the project is no longer as active and popular.

Alternatively, if you see a strong and engrained community, then this is a good indication that the project will continue to grow from users adding new user-generated content and evangelizing the overall adoption of the project.

Buying

Now that you've assessed the market, you might feel ready to start purchasing properties. One of the first steps is to set up a budget and short-list a number of properties you would like to bid on.

In terms of deciding a budget, it helps to know what you want to do with your investment and even find value where others don't. Moses Kagan, a Californian real estate manager, talks about constructing a differentiated lens: "a different way of looking at the world, specifically a different way of looking at assets, such that you see an asset that everyone else can see, and you have a way of looking at that asset that generates more return than everyone else does. Once you have a differentiated lens, you are like a kid in the candy store because you can just buy stuff that is on the market."

For you, maybe this "differentiated lens" is developing an exclusive venue that profits from being secluded and far away from the busy thoroughfares of virtual stores and public places, like a virtual Burning Man concert venue. Alternatively, maybe you are willing to pay more for a premium location because you are creating a business that relies on foot traffic, such as a meeting spot or art gallery. Other times, having a very small plot is perfect for what you want, i.e. leasing out billboards.

When it comes to the actual buying part, properties are typically sold on an auction bidding basis within a restricted period of time. When bidding on your first property, try to err on the conservative side and be ready to miss out on your first or second property offer.

If you are buying virtual land on a secondary marketplace, it makes sense to purchase a property at floor price (the lowest price for that asset category type). Purchasing land in the middle of the market can be more nuanced and susceptible to over-pricing, and unless you truly understand the market, there is more risk that you will overpay for that asset.

While less common, it's also possible to devise a direct handover of a property over the blockchain without going through an open marketplace. This direct handover method is likely to occur more often in the future as diseased owners pass their virtual property to family members or other benefactors.

APPENDIX: GETTING STARTED

Discord

As an instant messaging and digital distribution platform, Discord is one of the primary communication hubs for decentralized platforms and blockchain projects. You can use Discord to communicate via voice call, video call, messaging, as well as send files in private chats and form communities called "servers".

All of the major virtual world projects have a Discord channel as well as a series of servers for targeted conversations, including land servers for discussing virtual property, art servers, and even servers for other languages such as Korean and French. These servers are a great source of information and provide a valuable place to ask questions.

In the Decentraland land server, for example, you can find landowners wishing to sell or rent their land and other members looking to rent or buy land. In addition, each of the major virtual worlds has a Discord server dedicated to answering common questions for newcomers and technical queries regarding SDK and animation capabilities.

Naturally, you should always exercise vigilance in order to avoid potential scams shared in Discord servers, including suspicious external links, and never disclose information that might jeopardize the security of your digital wallet or other private property.

Wallet

Whether it's bidding on your first virtual property, receiving funds for a gig in the metaverse, or buying the latest avatar accessory, at some stage you will need to register a digital wallet. Additionally, you will sometimes need a digital wallet in order to log in and collect items, experience, or karma inside some virtual worlds.

At the time of writing, the most common wallet for interacting with Ethereum-based platforms is a browser extension wallet called MetaMask. Using your MetaMask wallet, you will be able to send and receive Ethereum-based coins including Ether (ETH), MANA, CUBES, SAND, etc., to purchase and hold NFTs, as well as log into Ethereum-based worlds.

MetaMask is available with Google Chrome, Firefox, Brave, and Edge browsers. To download MetaMask, first go to metamask.io or your browser store, such as the Chrome Store, and download the official MetaMask extension. From there, follow the wallet setup instructions.

When you first install and open MetaMask, it will issue you a randomly generated 12-word seed phrase. It's crucial that you store those 12 words somewhere safe. This information has the potential to unlock the full contents of your wallet, so it's very important that you make sure this seed phrase is safe and secure. If anything ever happens to your computer or your MetaMask account, as long as you have your 12-word seed phrase, there is no need to worry, as all your account details and funds will be recoverable. It's recommended that you write down and store the seed phrase in a safe place (most people recommend something like a fireproof safe) and not save the seed phrase to a digital device, which may be susceptible to hacking.

Next, add MetaMask to your browser tab in the top-right if it has not appeared there automatically.

Look for the fox icon in your browser extension section or add by clicking on the three dots on the right

When you first log in to MetaMask, you will be asked whether or not you want MetaMask to act as your default browser for accessing DApps (decentralized applications or programs that exist and run on a blockchain or peer-to-peer network). Selecting "Yes" means that every time you click on a link requesting access to your digital wallet, it will open via MetaMask and you can log in without ever having to take any extra signup steps. This essentially makes using DApps as easy as using normal mobile apps on your smartphone.

In terms of security, it's important to recognize that MetaMask is an online wallet, which is exposed to more potential security risks than hardware wallets and other forms of cold storage for storing your crypto holdings. Phishing attacks (fraudulent communications that appear to come from a reputable source) are one of the common risks facing MetaMask wallet holders.

Holding coins in your MetaMask is therefore not recommended for long-term storage. Please conduct your own research in order to best secure your digital funds.

Transferring Funds

To load up your MetaMask wallet with funds, you can either send Ethereum-based coins from a cryptocurrency exchange (such as Coinbase, Kraken, Binance, or Gemini) or from someone you know who has a wallet and who wishes to send funds to you (for business, work, donation, or another purpose).

To receive funds to your MetaMask wallet, you will need to share your wallet's ENS (Ethereum name service), which represents your Ethereum account and which also acts as your cross-platform web3 username and profile. By default, the ENS domain consists of a 42-character hexadecimal address that looks something   like   this: 0x8155e981BCeCDEE4f2b77db16d48Dbd2E6d18E62

Note that you can also purchase your own custom ENS domain at https://ens.domains/ for as low as 0.001 ETH (5 USD as of late 2021) per year plus gas fees, which for the time being, far exceeds the actual cost of the actual ENS domain. Note that you can only have one primary ENS domain per Ethereum account, which you can change at any time. This means, that while you can have two ENS domains, only one ENS domain can be linked to your Ethereum account at one time, and any other domains are inactive unless they are linked to another Ethereum account that you possess. Also, keep in mind that you can buy and sell ENS domains on secondary markets including OpenSea.

Lastly, in terms of selecting a cryptocurrency exchange to purchase tokens, you will need to factor in what coins the exchange offers (i.e. as of 2021 Coinbase does not offer SAND and CUBES), eligibility requirements based on what country you reside in and/or your tax location, and whether you are eligible to wire/transfer fiat (i.e. USD, GBP, AUD) to an exchange to purchase cryptocurrencies. In general, you want to avoid buying coins using a credit card due to the higher transaction fees. You will also need to factor in exchange fees based on your preferred payment method and other policies such as security and ease of use.

OpenSea

After topping up your MetaMask or equivalent wallet with Ethereum-based coins (and not Bitcoin), you'll be able to make purchases on the marketplace of decentralized worlds or a secondary market like OpenSea.

OpenSea offers a peer-to-peer marketplace for buying and selling virtual assets including virtual land, art, avatar names, avatar skins, ENS domains, and other collectibles as long as they have been minted or transferred to the Ethereum blockchain or the Polygon sidechain[28]. OpenSea added support for Polygon (formally known as Matic), which is a layer 2 scaling solution built on the Ethereum blockchain, to make buying and selling on the platform more cost-effective. Specifically, Polygon helps to combat the high gas fees of using Ethereum, especially during periods of high network congestion. In fact, for the year 2021, OpenSea was the largest consumer of gas on the Ethereum network.

To search for NFTs on OpenSea, you can type in the project name or digital artist and check that it is has a blue checkmark to ensure it's a verified collection. OpenSea has a number of filters you can use to search for items based on your set budget as well as purchase type (auction or buy now), specific blockchain, and currency of the sale. You will typically find that most items on OpenSea are priced in Ether (ETH) but are also sometimes priced in a local token such as SAND, and not in the sidechain Polygon.

While it's possible to add ETH to OpenSea using their fiat to cryptocurrency conversion service, this option is typically more expensive than the same service on cryptocurrency exchanges and may not be available to users from all countries or regions.

Note that you can also convert one coin into another, such as Bitcoin into ETH, using the MetaMask wallet, the cryptocurrency exchange where you purchased and are currently holding coins, or on a third-party platform such as Uniswap and OpenSea. Be careful to conduct a comparison of conversion fees based on the platform you use to convert coins.

Ether (ETH) can also be exchanged for wrapped Ether (WETH), which is used to bid in auction sales. As standard ETH was programmed for transactions to be authorized immediately and not in the future, it cannot be used to submit bids and participate in auctions on OpenSea. Standard ETH and other coins, such as MANA and SAND, can though be used to purchase NFTs on OpenSea using the buy now method[29], which is an instant transaction.

Wrapped ETH, meanwhile, is programmed to allow buyers to make pre-authorized bids that can be fulfilled at a later day without any further action from the bidder. This time delay allows you to bid during an auction for a future transaction that may or may not take place (several hours, days, or weeks into the future), which is not possible using standard ETH. If you win an auction, the wrapped ETH will be sent to the seller, and if your bid is unsuccessful, the full amount of wrapped ETH will be returned to your wallet.

Standard ETH and wrapped ETH are worth exactly the same in value, so there is no price difference to worry about. Standard ETH is denoted by a black Ethereum icon, whereas WETH is denoted by a pink Ethereum icon.

You can conveniently convert standard ETH into wrapped ETH directly within OpenSea or via another exchange platform for a modest fee after signing for the transaction within your Meta-Mask wallet. However, keep in mind that it's normally cheaper to convert ETH into WETH than it is to convert WETH back into ETH.

Selling on OpenSea

First-time sellers listing on OpenSea must pay two transaction gas fees to set up their seller account, one to authorize their wallet to conduct sell orders and the other to allow OpenSea access to their NFT item when a sale occurs, which are both a one-time fee and thus only paid once.

NFT transactions made on the Ethereum network are also subject to gas fees. For fixed-price items, the buyer pays for the gas
fee, and for auctions or buyer-initiated price offers, the seller is
responsible for paying the gas fee in order to accept. During times
of high network congestion, gas fees can be prohibitively expensive, sometimes more expensive than the actual item sold. Gas
also cannot be purchased in advance of a transaction and used
later. It is only available at live spot prices.

In addition, each sale on OpenSea is currently subject to a 2.5%
service fee (comparatively low for this industry) and a potential
royalty fee to the NFT creator[30], which is often 10% or less.

When receiving bids from potential buyers, make sure the bid
is issued in the correct currency, as sometimes it's possible to bid
in multiple currencies. One USD, for example, is not the same as
one ETH in terms of value. To avoid low bid offers, you can set a
reserve price that implements a minimal purchase amount that
must be reached in order for a sale to occur. Auctions are also ex-
tended by 10 minutes for every bid made during the last minutes
of the auction in order to avoid late-ditch attempts to snatch an
auctioned item.

Tips For Using OpenSea

- When assessing NFT projects, it's good to see a high number of owners (which means strong and diffused demand
  not relying on several whales) and comparatively low supply (that produces scarcity).
- Be cognizant of the multiple branches of volatility to owning NFTs. This includes the market volatility of the NFT
  itself, secondly the volatility of the coin (i.e. ETH, MANA,
  etc.), and the volatility for the parent token in the case of
  ERC-20 tokens such as MANA and SAND which operate on
  the Ethereum network. In addition, unlike currency tokens

that can be sold openly on an exchange at market rates without the "yes or no" approval of the exchange, NFTs are not as liquid; you need an individual buyer to explicitly agree to the sale, which may be difficult to find during a rampant selloff.

· You can usually receive a better price and avoid gas fees by submitting a bid in wrapped ETH rather than clicking the "Buy Now" option where you as the buyer are responsible for paying the full price as well as the gas fees. However, this approach may not always work because the seller must accept your bid and it also takes more time for a sale to occur.

· Sometimes the seller will include their Discord contact details on their listing. This enables you to talk with them directly on Discord (which is not possible on OpenSea) and negotiate a better price as well as develop a buyer/seller relationship. For example, after negotiating the purchase of land on Decentraland from a seller, I was able to ask them some questions via Discord about building an art gallery, and the seller kindly offered me a free 3D gallery model that I could install on my land.

· Note that you can bid on NFTs listed on OpenSea that are not listed for sale using wrapped ETH. After the NFT is sold (through an auction or an instant purchase), it will still be viewable on OpenSea and anyone can make a bid to purchase, which the current buyer can choose to accept or ignore. In other words, an NFT such as virtual land or an ENS domain does not have to be listed for sale in order for you to submit an offer to the NFT owner using your wrapped ETH. To look up the collections of other NFT holders, you can enter their Ethereum address into the search bar on OpenSea.

· If the price seems too good to be true, then it's quite likely to be a scam or what's known in the industry as a rug pull.

· To avoid scams when purchasing on OpenSea, always check that the NFT you are purchasing is from a verified collection with the blue tick icon next to the creator name.

Created by SomniumSpace ✅

FURTHER RESOURCES

The following are important resources that have influenced my own understanding of the metaverse and are recommended resources for you to explore further.

Snow Crash (Book)

Merging Sumerian mythology with computer programming, Neal Stephenson explores the relationship between the real world and virtual reality in the cyberpunk fiction that inspired the metaverse concept and the publication of this book. Neal's attention to detail and wicked style of prose will leave your head reeling in sections but the book's jutted structure will just as easily lose you in other chapters. Nonetheless, this book is a must-read for inspiration and insight for the future.

Ready Player One (Book)

Published in 2011 by debut author Ernest Cline, the science fiction novel is another popular fictional story that takes place between the real world and the metaverse. The story is set in 2045 and follows Wade Watts on his search for an Easter egg in a worldwide virtual reality game. The novel was adapted for film and released in 2018 film directed by Steven Spielberg. For me, the book is an easier read than Snow Crash but less applicable for understanding the economics and mechanics of the metaverse era we are now entering.

The Metaverse Primer (Blog)

Matthew Ball is an American venture capitalist and via his blog matthewball.vc, he outlines the important technologies crucial for building the metaverse. This resource is an outstanding reference point for understanding the technical and theoretical requirements of building the metaverse from a macro investor perspective.

DCLBlogger (YouTube)

DCLBlogger is an Australian YouTuber, blogger, co-founder of the Metakey project, and investor of NFT's. For a guided tour of Decentraland and insights on how he quit his job so he could find more time to flip virtual properties and amass a digital fortune, check out his YouTube channel as well as his Twitter (@**DCLBlogger**) and various podcast interviews.

Play-to-Earn (Documentary)

Filmed in January 2021, this mini-documentary about Axie Infinity in the Philippines was inspired by an article written by Coindesk columnist, Leah Callon-Butler (also the screenwriter and narrator of the documentary). Leah's original article tells the story of a young family in a rural province north of Manila that took shifts playing Axie Infinity up to 20 hours each day in order to earn an income.

https://www.youtube.com/watch?v=Yo-BrASMHU4

The Augmented Workforce: How Artificial Intelligence, Augmented Reality, and 5G Will Impact Every Dollar You Make (Book)

The Augmented Workforce by Cathy Hackl and John Buzzell is a new book examining the role that new technologies will play in the future of work. The authors explore how AR, AI, VR, IoT, and 5G technologies are being adopted by organizations to improve the way they do business. This book doesn't directly cover the metaverse but still provides interesting insights on the supporting technologies and business cases. Cathy Hackl is also worth following for her excellent insight on the metaverse on other media including Twitter (@**CathyHackl**).

Mastering Ethereum: Building Smart Contracts and DApps (Textbook)

Authored by industry experts Andreas Antonopoulos and Gavin Wood and published by O'Reilly Media, this is a technical introduction to Ethereum for those willing to dive into the mechanics of tokens, smart contracts, web3, gas fees, as well as programming language fundamentals for creating decentralized applications.

Podcasts of Note

Future of the Metaverse, Cathy Hackl
Modern Finance, Kevin Rose
Talk2Much Podcast, Sina Pahlevan
The Delphi Podcast, Tom Shaughnessy
Welcome to the Metaverse, MetaverseLuke
The Metaverse Podcast, Jamie Burke
Hello Metaverse, Annie Zhang
Real Vision Crypto

Ingram Content Group UK Ltd.
Milton Keynes UK
UKHW020748130323
418477UK00014B/2137